Systemic Knowledge Management and Social Challenges
Systemisches Wissensmanagement und soziale Herausforderungen

Innovatives Wissensmanagement
Innovative Knowledge Management

Band 5

Zur Qualitätssicherung und Peer Review der vorliegenden Publikation

Die Qualität der in dieser Reihe erscheinenden Arbeiten wird vor der Publikation durch externe, von der Herausgeberschaft benannte Gutachter geprüft.

Notes on the quality assurance and peer review of this publication

Prior to publication, the quality of the work published in this series is reviewed by external referees appointed by the editorship.

Bernhard F. Seyr (ed.)

Systemic Knowledge Management and Social Challenges

Systemisches Wissensmanagement und soziale Herausforderungen

PETER LANG
Lausanne - Berlin - Bruxelles - Chennai - New York - Oxford

Bibliographic information published by the Deutsche Nationalbibliothe
The German National Library lists this publication in the German National Bibliography; detailed bibliographic data is available on the Internet at http://dnb.d-nb.de.

Library of Congress Cataloging-in-Publication Data
A CIP catalog record for this book has been applied for at the Library of Congress.

ISSN 2699-6324
ISBN 978-3-631-90794-8 (Print)
E-ISBN 978-3-631-90798-6 (E-PDF)
E-ISBN 978-3-631-90799-3 (EPUB)
DOI 10.3726/b21143

Published by Peter Lang GmbH, Berlin, Deutschland

info@peterlang.com - www.peterlang.com

Peter Lang · Berlin · Bruxelles · Lausanne · New York · Oxford

This publication has been peer reviewed.

Inhalt

Autorenverzeichnis – List of Authors

in alphabetischer Reihenfolge der Familiennamen – in alphabetical order of the last names

Ing. Martina Chalupová, PhD
MSc from the University of Economics in Prague; PhD from the Czech University of Life Sciences in Prague (CZ), where she currently works at the Management Department as assistant professor. Her long-time focus includes internationalization, being also responsible for the short-term mobilities within the International Business Network.
E-Mail: chalupovam@pef.czu.cz

Daniela Hofmann, PhD
Doktorat für Management und Organisationswissenschaften der Universität Sopron (H); Rechtsanwältin und seit fast 15 Jahren Hochschuldozentin für Wirtschaftsrecht und Wettbewerbsrecht an der Fontys University of Applied Sciences, Venlo (NL).
E-Mail: d.hofmann@fontys.nl

Prof. Raja Suzana Raja Kasim, PhD
Postgraduate Diploma in Entrepreneurship at University of Cambridge (UK); Professor of entrepreneurship at the University Malaysia Kelantan; research and consulting focuses: Islamic personal knowledge management, strategic entrepreneurship and sustainability, social innovation, entrepreneurship education and strategic management. She passionately works to improve the pedagogy of entrepreneurship education and startup for youth living in the marginalised communities.
E-Mail: rajasuzana@umk.edu.my

Dkfm. Norbert Klein
Direktor für den Bereich Interne Revision bei einer mittelgroßen Sparkasse, seit Juni 2022 auch externer Gutachter für Bachelor-Abschlüsse an der Fontys University of Applied Sciences, Venlo (NL).
E-Mail: klein.buettgen@dg-email.de

Prof. Dr. Dr. habil. Klaus Oestreicher
Professor emeritus of the Nyangani Virtual University, Harare (ZW) – Salzburg (A); Fellow with the British Higher Education Academy; Chartered Marketer and Fellow with the Chartered Institute of Marketing, and Member and Accredited Practitioner with the Chartered Institute of Public Relations. Areas of research: disruptive innovation and their economic and societal impact, corporate strategic development. Before he held academic senior positions with Grandes Écoles in France, and a university in the UK, and he also served as Visiting Professor with universities in Asia, Africa, and Europe. Before his academic career, he was a member of the board of multinational German and US corporations for nearly 25 years.

Nurul Azreen Salleh
Researcher and postgraduate researcher at the Faculty of Entrepreneurship and Business, University Malaysia Kelantan; research focuses: Islamic personal knowledge management and positive youth development; current research on building an *insaniah* (humanitarian) model for at-risk youth into entrepreneurship.
E-Mail: a20d0239f@siswa.umk.edu.my

Tit. Univ.-Prof. Dr. Dr. Dr. habil. Bernhard F. Seyr
Doctoral degrees in management and social sciences as well as in education sciences, habilitation in economics and organisation sciences. Director General of the European Association for Knowledge Economy – EURECO; business consultant; certified expert at the court of the Land Salzburg (A); Honorary Professor at the University of Sopron (H).
E-Mail: seyr@seyr.at

Marie Sitter, MSc
Senior Manager at Andreus Management Consulting (D)
E-Mail: MarieCSitter@aol.de

PhDr. František Smrčka, PhD
studied Physics and Basics of Technology at the Faculty of Education of Masaryk University in Brno, where he also received the degree of Doctor of Pedagogical Sciences. He also studied computer technology at the Faculty of Informatics of Masaryk University in Brno. At Mendel University of Agriculture and Forestry in Brno, Faculty of Economics, he obtained a PhD. At present he is assistant professor at the Department of Technical Studies at the College of Polytechnics,

Jihlava (CZ). He mainly deals with the programming of web applications and the design of information systems.
E-Mail: frantisek.smrcka@vspj.cz

Dr. Patrick Szillat
Manager of Postgraduate Programmes; Research Chair Cross-Border Business Development – both at Fontys University of Applied Sciences, Venlo (NL).
E-Mail: p.szillat@fontys.nl

Doc. Dr., Ing. Jan Voracek, CSc.
MSc and PhD degrees from the Brno Technical University, Czech Republic, all in Technical Cybernetics; associate professor at the Department of Technical Studies, College of Polytechnics, Jihlava (CZ); special fields of interest: computer simulation of complex socio-technical systems and knowledge management.
E-Mail: jan.voracek@vspj.cz

Editorial

Band 5 der Schriftenreihe *Innovatives Wissensmanagement* setzt seine Schwerpunkte auf systemische Betrachtungen der Ressource Wissen sowie auf aktuelle Herausforderungen im sozialen Bereich und innovative Lösungen.

So ist das erste Kapitel dem systemischen Denken betreffend den Aufbau und den Erhalt von Kompetenzen und Fähigkeiten in Organisationen gewidmet. Der Autor kommt zu dem systemtheoretischen Schluss, dass es einer ganzheitlichen Betrachtung der Problematik bedarf, denn einzelne Faktoren isoliert zu betrachten, greift zu kurz. Der zweite Beitrag befasst sich mit dem Thema der wahrgenommenen Authentizität der sozialen Verantwortung von Unternehmen im Zusammenhang mit dem Konsumverhalten. Im Zuge dessen wird das soziale und ökologische Problem von „Fast Fashion" beleuchtet. Kapitel 3 widmet sich innovativen Systemen zum Austausch von dringenden Informationen zur Unterstützung der Internationalisierung an Hochschulen. Dieser Beitrag ist technisch-organisatorisch angelegt und entwirft ein Kommunikationsmodell. Kapitel 4 ist weniger technisch, dafür mehr interkulturell und philosophisch ausgerichtet und bezieht sich auf Praktiken des Wissensmanagements in der islamischen Welt mit Bezug zu jugendlichen Randgruppen. Ebenfalls Kapitel 5 ist auf ein soziales Thema fokussiert, und zwar auf das Ehrenamt. Es wird dort der Frage nachgegangen, inwieweit das Wissen über Risiken ehrenamtlich Tätige dabei beeinflusst, Vereinsfunktionen zu übernehmen. Das abschließende Kapitel 6 ist demgegenüber wieder managementwissenschaftlich orientiert und stellt das derzeit vieldiskutierte Thema der agilen Führung durch Ziele im Zusammenhang mit OKR (Objectives and Key Results) in den Vordergrund. Dabei wird die Thematik anwendungsorientiert mit Bezug zum Sparkassensektor betrachtet.

Salzburg, im September 2023

Der Herausgeber:

Tit. Univ.-Prof. Dr. Dr. Dr. habil. Bernhard F. Seyr

Generaldirektor der Europäischen Gesellschaft für Wissensökonomie (EURECO)

Klaus Oestreicher

1. Competence: Thinking in Systems

Abstract: Knowledge is an essential part of the organisational system. Vertically and horizontally embedded into organised processes and activities, knowledge furthers competence which contributes to progress and viability. Understanding an organisation as a system and attributing to knowledge the meaning of a subsystem in its own right bears causal consequences. In systems' general understanding of everything is connected with everything, knowledge enters interdependencies and interactions within and beyond the system of the own organisation. To manage a knowledge building and storing system, competence needs to be a meaningful strategic layer, which delivers value for the organisation. This means that knowledge and competence are organised interactors for improving the systemic effectiveness within an organisation.

By a view on the multidimensional and multi-layered interactions within an organisation, the chapter adopts a causal-consequential, hence methodological view on the understanding of knowledge as an organisational subsystem. The view is further extended to competence and argues that interconnections and interdependencies with both living and non-living species of the system are leading to an ecosystem with its own constituents. The chapter also examines the role of knowledge and its closely related components as an integrated systemic interface of an organisation which effectively supports the organisational performance.

Keywords: Knowledge, competence, system, ecosystem, organisational complexity

1.1. Introduction: Everything Is Connected with Everything

By thinking in strategy, knowledge offers direction and progress for societies and economies. However, knowledge is much more than a strategy-monolithic constituent. It is, as the following discussion will argue, an influential part of a multi-layered systemic architecture. In it, competence, capabilities, skills, and abilities are playing an additional interwoven and interacting role by forming supportive dimensions. Altogether, they are building systemic structures which need effectiveness for maximising outcomes. Interdependent and interactive flows of knowledge-based energy depend on efficiently structured connections for the underlying cycles of organisational processes.

Before delving into the more detailed argumentation, essential defining factors need clarification. Human developments depend on both individual and collective memories, actual experiences, and future-oriented curiosity, which can be, e.g., cultural, societal, scientific, and economic. New experience and knowledge are gained by structured and unstructured processes; in intentional and/or coincidental, in systematic and/or chaotic form. The collective wisdom and experiences of humanity are organised, stored, and conserved in physical and virtual databases of public and private organisations, services, and by individuals. In the last decades, much effort was put into the retrospective digitisation of existing knowledge for easiness and speed of access, and to not be lost to conflicts and natural disasters so easily as before. The key objective is the accessibility, availability of knowledge, and, as well, the affordability of its sharing. Cumulative effects can improve working and living conditions multidimensionally. This introduces three system-oriented factors, for which the systematic of the corresponding management is key regarding the effectiveness of human and other paths of progress. I.e., the effectiveness of the resulting architecture depends on strong and global connections, which can form multi-layered (1) hubs, (2) nodes, and (3) interactive lines for mutual exchange. In the daily routine, the often-contrasting impression is that agents' holistic view on the systematic handling of knowledge and their fundamental systemic understanding remains far too often underdeveloped. It frequently reads as if siloed structures do exist and are, in systems' terms, placed all over the landscape of organisations and individuals. However, instead of artificially isolated fields, pathways of specialisation, or similar, many connections do naturally exist. It may be said, in Morin's (2005) explanation, they auto-exist. Those connections need organisation by knowledgeable management, for that they can deliver process-energy beyond the own boundaries. Based on long-term ethnographic research, the argument is that while connections are naturally available, in organisational contexts, they are too frequently avoided or not immediately discovered. This defines a lack of necessary competence.

A globalised and democratised organisation of knowledge connects various types of human beings through similar and/or various interests and objectives, and it serves to connect on various dimensions for finding new outcomes. People with people and people with artefacts of knowledge. People also create new connections of artefact ↔ artefact character. All connections own the fundamental power to create new knowledge. Contributors are directing towards a rather special system, the ecosystem. For Clapham (cited in Campbell et al., 2008) and Odum (1971), an ecosystem is formed by all interacting organisms, which are living and interacting in a specific area. To these organisms add all those non-living physical components of the environment with which these organisms interact (cf. Moore, 1993). The purpose of the resulting interacting system is that a flow of energy leads to clearly defined trophic structure and biodiversity and material cycles. By the more general perspectives, the central focus is synthesised in the systemic view. It starts with the suggestion that, like other phenomena, knowledge and its directly interacting parallel components are following systems' iron principles. Firstly, everything, which means knowledge in this context, is connected with all other knowledge. This central definition extends by using the principle of Bronfenbrenner (1979). Bronfenbrenner's multi-circular artefact allows placing knowledge as one layer of the bigger system of human and natural existences, which "auto"-connects beyond knowledge:

Everything is connected with everything.

The further argument suggests that knowledge is a key and a strategic systemic layer at the same time. The next connected aspect is that a systemic approach provides structure and order. By the adoption of a second systemic principle, systems provide organising structures, i.e., a functioning system must be organised. Actively and passively, organisms interacting in a viable system are collaborating to establish order in which the system's organisms or species can live and prosper. In logic-causal translation that links to Pirsig's (cited in Meadows, 2008, n. p.) core assumption that "[i]f a factory is torn down, but the rationality which produced it, is left standing, then that rationality will simply produce another factory. If a revolution destroys a government, but the systematic patterns of thought that produced that government are left intact, then those patterns will reproduce themselves. … There's so much talk about the system. And so little understanding." This involves knowledge and that in managed form. On the other hand, "little understanding" draws attention to the opposite, a lack of knowledge. Witzel (2009) cites Casson, who concluded for the economic world, already in the year 1931, that in both the managerial and operational side of a business, actors had little or no knowledge about what they were really doing. The consequence then is that if there is not enough organisation, and the organisation of forward-leading knowledge, the important constituent of effectiveness risks to become a matter of chance. As causal question of reflection then follows: how can knowledge be organised in systematic form, then? One, which is also following principles of effectiveness?

Systemic knowledge and its management are organised structures in general, or ones in the need of becoming organised in process-giving structures, which the following discourse is not limiting to an economic or business form. The thought leads to the third defining principle. A system is alive when it produces processes, providing an interdependency which owns circular and reciprocal effects. Todeva (2007, p. 7) connects organisational behaviour to contingency theory as "one of the predecessors of the knowledge-based view and has argued about the same dynamic adaptation between an organisation and its environment" condensing that everything is connected with everything.

1.2. Knowledge Management and the Competence-System

Witzel (2009) writes about the coherent system of management, which needs the practice and capabilities of acting managers. Both are essential systemic nodes contributing to gain and build competence, by an economic perspective, but as well beyond. In addition to capabilities, which are starting on the simpler level of abilities, competence forms an essential foundation for strategic navigation in challenging contextual settings. Nevertheless, it means to establish the meaningful combination of the full set comprising abilities, skills, and knowledge. This helps to build and enhance capabilities for the establishment of an organisation's competence base. Knowledge, "because knowledge creation capability relies on exchanging and combining information and knowledge among organisational members" (Smith et al. cited in Su et al., 2015, p. 3). The starting point is a narrow but complex circle of elements. The competence base of an organisation owns significance in any form of it. It opens options for systematic improvements, and beyond improvement it supports innovation (Su et al., 2015). A serious problem zone can be found in the controversial debate on knowledge, abilities, skills, and capabilities, but as well competence. They are terms and notions, which are too often used in interchangeable and confusing ways. There is no generally uniform understanding building a clear or precisely defining taxonomy. Such discussion would undoubtedly contribute more arguments, but it will not lead to a meaningful outcome of an accepted taxonomy. Therefore, the chosen brief approach is following practice-orientation and use of the common understanding, which is found in many dictionaries and organisations' language as well (see table 1.1).

Table 1.1: Definitions

Ability	A person having the means or skills to do something
Skill	The ability to do something well
Capability	A person having the possibility to do something well
Knowledge	Is based on facts, information, and skills acquired through experience or education; it comprises the theoretical or practical understanding of a subject.

It is not essential here to discuss each of the per se too simplistic definitions in more depth. The differentiation between ability and skill suggests the difference between the understanding that one person has the basic ability to do something, while the skilled person can do it much better. If the person then has the possibility to really do it well, they are capable. That reads as three degrees of comparison. In a deeper understanding, the problem of non-systematic starts already here, and it widely ignores that all are embedded in the same system. One can be a capable person without task-related skills, may even have little ability to do such task themselves, but has the capability and/or power to organise that it gets done well. That then forms a different possibility to do something well by facilitation. This constitutes a differentiation between actively or passively doing the job. But if passively doing it, the person enables its fulfilment actively. At least, it leads to a form of differentiating understanding that there are two layers of capabilities: Luhmann's (2016) systems-based "distinction between distinctions". The one layer is the person who can physically do it well; the other layer is that of the person, who can organise that others having the physical skills are enabled to do it well. Both layers can also be united in one person. In the more philosophical meaning, this can be understood as a complexity in its own right; i.e., "the whole is in the part, which is in the whole" (Morin, 2005, p. 101). What comes to light is a first path towards thinking in systems. Such impression is not only guided by the omnipresence of connected elements but as well by the need to organise complexity for the reason of making it manageable, i.e., functional for the avoidance of systemic malfunctioning. One form of opposing pole is to structure for the creation of synergies through interdependence and interconnections which are part of the organisation, and, in addition, between the organisation and the environment. It means understanding (the) organisation as an organism. Classical and humanistic theories understand organisational behaviour, organisational structure, or managerial practice (prediction and control). It forms a machine. Systems theory instead opposes the understanding as machine, which is constituted on the factors of prediction and control (Anonymous, 2001). It views an organisation in general, i. e. , in form of an organism. The functioning and healthy organisation needs both. An organisation must own the capability to balance organism and machine forming a further whole of the part, which is in the whole. It is the organised set of elements standing in interrelations. As a system, it needs those who can physically execute work well, and important for systems' functionality, it also needs those, who can organise that the first ones have the possibility to execute good work.

Such line from ability to capability enhances further when knowledge is added. "In the business context, knowledge is defined as information that is relevant, actionable, and based at least partially on experience" (Leonhard & Sensiper, 1998, p. 113). This describes the organism on microsystem level which knows and understands, but also has a physical capability in addition, why something should be done in certain ways and not others to result in a good outcome. While Leonhard et al.'s combination makes sense, by omni-connected thinking in systems, it can also be two (or more) living organisms, persons, then organised as part of a mutual impulse-giving connection. However, as the ongoing controversial discussion and much research demonstrates, these arguments may be reasonable and understandable, but neither they are complete, nor do they anyhow embrace the many complexities adjacent to them. They remain a simplicity within complexity (cf. Morin, 2005).

These reflections are introducing a web of underlying complexities which thinking in the competence-based system faces. They extend further when the work on competence of Yuvaraj (2011) is explored. He suggests extended differentiation between competence and competency. In his view, competence is more related to what an organisation owns, and he attributes competency to a person. For him, competence is then process-oriented, competency result-oriented (Yuvaraj, 2011). Balogun, Hope Hailey and Viardot (2005) are making the same differentiation in form of organisational and personal competences. They add the further layer of important interconnectedness by stating that the personal competence of a member of staff can exceed the level of the existing organisational competence. E.g., tensions can be caused by the fact that what a manager considers as important or necessary cannot be realised, because the rest of the system is not able, capable, or prepared to follow. The existing system's competence may become overstressed, which frequently happens when confronted with radical innovation. Radical innovation typically differs from the existing competence-base in which the completely new way of thinking and doing things is not embedded or existing: the anti-established systemic process disruption which requires new knowledge and experiences in form of capabilities and/or skills. This differentiation is of explanatory nature and should be seen as another or additional form of what Luhmann (2016) introduced as a system's distinction between distinctions. In this vein, we are returning to Yuvaraj's terms and follow them a little further. This leads to the interpretation of the causal sequence as those capabilities and knowledge, which are forming the individuals' competencies whose collective input creates the competence of an organisation. This can result in three different levels (see table 1.2):

Table 1.2: Levels of competence

1.	Organisational competence	>	individual competency
2.	Organisational competence	<	individual competency
3.	Organisational competence	=/≈	individual competency

Of course, this must be seen subject-specifically. The organisational competence comprises all fields, while typically the individual level will cover one or a few subject areas. However, the need for coherence within the entire system and for balance can be recognised. The more individual competency levels are balanced with the collective result of the organisational one, the better and more frictionless the system can operate. Adaptations become easier, adjustments faster, and if the system integrates renewal and updates of competencies, agility and flexibility will support longer-term viability. The balance of organisational competence supports its equilibrium with the surrounding ecosystem. With reference to the knowledge-based organisation organising a systematically organised competence framework connects for mutually beneficial outcomes. What should never be forgotten is that endogenous and especially exogenous contexts are subject to change. I.e., as concluded, a competence-base is transitional as well. I.e., competence on organisational and personal level is subject to adaptation and renewal to keep the system operational, hence alive. As long as processes of the system are created and recreated, it is kept alive.

These thoughts on competence and its elements serve to clarify that the competence-based system is not a phenomenon which provides clearly definable components and stable order. Instead, it offers many options for controversial discussion. Yet, the competence-based system can be seen as important for progress and viability. Freiling (2004) posits that competence is important for sustaining competitive advantage, which contributes to both. What the Theory of Constraints holds seems never to be distant. As soon as one bottleneck of thinking in systems is dealt with, the next one emerges (cf. Cox III & Schleier, 2010). Therefore, what is the competence-based system's characteristics? Which share does competence own within and also as part of the organisational main system and organised structure of the organisation, especially when seen as a contributing layer to strategic logic? Complexity remains a permanent companion. While Morin (2005) holds that complexity is the opposite of simplicity, thinking in systems and through this, effective action creates new knowledge through changes in the system. It facilitates the management of existing knowledge by adaptation.

For the systems approach, competence is a subsystem, hence a contributor of values for what can be signified as the main system of the organisation. It organises processes which have competence and adjacent factors as central concern. Speaking about the systemic organisation of competence means the delivery of optimised results, too, if managed strategically. Simplified, a strategic understanding of a system cannot work without a specific level of competencies which are based on profound knowledge. Through these, effective and competent foundations for the guidance of advantageous operations are developed. That means systemic coherence for which a systematic management orientation becomes a decisive supplier and focus. This constitutes the connection that management based on knowledge delivers additional impact when it is systematic at the same time. But what precisely means systematic management? An immediate answer to this has many options depending on individual emphases and also depends on the approach by the chosen field of knowledge. In the wider view, the coherence of a system suggests a general fit in which all parts and functions of the organisation are having the best-possible organised fit for enhanced impact. Systematic management, as simplified definition, follows a causal-consequential trajectory of effectiveness which is based on reliable competenc(i)es and trusted information. Its objective is to enable seamless operations of input →throughput →output and causes as little waste as possible. Maximisation of all resources and simultaneous reduction of scarcity is the ideal state of affairs of the coherent system. For the organisation it means a result of system-oriented best practice. Resource maximisation combined with maximised waste reduction is also an operational state of affairs which is quantifiable.

In internal processes of the organisation, introduced as inside-in perspective, and in the theoretical general view, the achievement of such state of affairs is rather difficult. This starts with the effect that not everything in an organisation can be directly quantified. They are much more than on (1) or off (0). Multiple contributors making the coherent system operational tend to be diverse. I.e., the coherence of the system depends on both quantitative and qualitative factors, without always or necessarily leading to an objective answer of right or wrong, or allowing the attribution of a value of achievement going beyond subjective impressions of the management. This knowledge is for competences not different than for other organisational processes. I.e., to evaluate what may be the perfect fit is difficult, transitional, and often enough open for debate. Systematic management also transforms two-dimensional organisational thinking, often ineffective today, to three-dimensional systems-orientation. Just as one example, a matrix is easily overstressed, due to the frequent neglect of an influential third variable (cf. Keidel, 2010). It starts, e.g., with the fine-tuning of ability, capability, and knowledge. Thus, systematic management needs informed ground, which comes in the form of a self-stabilising system-oriented triangle. The explanation is that nature must be based on triangles as the most stable geometric structure and being a set of three energy giving events getting critical proximity with [self-]stabilising effects (Fuller cited in Keidel, 2010). Stability makes systems, instability can destroy them.

What needs to be generally understood is that an organisation consists of many systems which all need to be managed individually and as a whole: architecture and artefact. How far the idea of systems reaches within these, and how deep thinking in systems is per se implicitly or explicitly embedded in organisational structures is outlined by Vakola, Soderquist and Prastacos (2007). They are also drawing attention to the difficulties to build a competence system in an organisation. Their study is on the internal difficulties to which naturally adds the exogenous dimension. No organisation acts in a vacuum. Thus, coherence with the external world must be part of the organisational systemic thinking, too: complexity is the opposite of simplicity (Morin, 2005). The manifold resulting difficulties and complexities are challenging especially smaller organisations. They often need more hands-on management and lack qualifications, which are allowing to think and manage in systems' ways. For big organisations, the challenges are not easier because the organisation of competences to build a multi-layered system are creating different types of complexities. Different internal cultures, differing or confronting organisational and/or individual interests, wider external contexts, or extended differing stakeholder demands are just a few of the challenges for both types. However, the argument is that experienced systemic *and* systematic management facilitates positive outcomes.

In this particular discussion, the essence is demonstrating that in addition to the main and further organisational systems the competence system is a (sub)system of special importance. All systems and organisational activities do profit from competence and its underlying knowledge. However, competence remains a more difficult element. Complexity in practice starts, but does not end with reliably differentiating competence, competency, skills, capabilities, knowledge. When it comes, in Yuvaraj's terms, to the differentiation between the firm's competence, which is based on its staff's competencies, the risk that what literature refers to as key competence is that it typically depends on competencies which members of staff are owning. Staff changes positions within the firm, staff joins an enterprise and leaves it. "Difficulties with the operation and implementation of competency management systems are mostly related to the complex and lengthy process required for identifying the appropriate competencies for an organisation and for building the appropriate competency model" (Athey et al. cited in Vakola et al., 2007, p. 260). In a volatile world, this creates difficulties to build a coherent system producing competence and to retain individual competencies. The result is a dynamic system or what Akiyama & Kaneko define as a "dynamical systems game … in which the game itself can change due to the influence of players' behaviours and states" (2000, p. 221). Akiyama et al. continue to explain that "the state of the game environment, the states of all the players, and the players' possible actions vary in time, and all of them are described by dynamical variables" (2000, p. 224). This does not only mean that there is a game between two or more competitors in form of entities or organisations, there further runs a parallel game inside organisations in which one of the dynamical elements is the competency of one or more members of staff. That can be a rare resource for the company, or the opposite, and it suggests two layers for the coherent system of management needing even more systematic to remain controllable: system as machine then (cf. Anonymous, 2001. In games theory's terms, the result is a complexity in its own right, the two-level game:

1. The exogenous layer which is played between two different organisations, typically and in economic settings to gain some sort of competitive advantages. Similar can be said about nations and national competitiveness as well.
2. The endogenous layer is played between the organisation itself and specific members of staff being in possession of rare competencies.

The instant logic is to keep such dynamics in equilibrium, cf. the Nash Equilibrium (cf. Heifetz, 2012). It forms a core challenge every day for which systematic management alone is not enough. Especially the side of general and situational human behaviour poses challenges, which are demanding specific competenc(i)es of cross-disciplinary nature. The requirement is that in this particular context systematic management has the competence to balance a permanently running two-level game best possibly. The game is played by exogenous players on one level, endogenous players on the other level, and by both at the same time. The game-theoretical objective is defining and reaching the objective of a state of organisation-stabilising coherence as the win set. It must be assumed that this effort is frequently subject to self-interests. This can make the balance within and for the system challenging and short-lived. The result must be expected to have a state of nearly permanent imperfectness. The extent of imperfectness will vary between the two levels of the simultaneous game. The situation can be described as a complex game of applied daily practice.

The more general view on systems will quickly lead to the discovery that they often operate and co-operate as two-level games. Thinking in systems suggests perceiving, the first dimension, an organised entity as the "non"-living part to which the species of human beings, the second dimension, are building the living equivalent. A major starting point for organising systematic and systemic management can be found here. One, which is subject to change, and one which experiences reorganisation and adaptation, as structures and/or contexts are changing. No system exists in eternity. In nature's triangular architecture, a third dimension is the competence to build such system (cf. Meadows, 2008), to maintain it, and to adapt when necessary. Correctly connected and supplied with sound knowledge, the competence base can support the system itself for that it can, in Morin's (2005) words, organise a level of self-development and auto-repair. "If we no longer conceive of a strict determinism but a universe where what is created, is created not only in chance, but in self-organising processes, that is to say where each system creates its own determinations and its own purposes, we can first understand, at a minimum, the autonomy, then we can begin to understand what it means to be subject" (Morin, 2005, p. 88). That means coherence in which the subject is the competency to deal with the subject of competence as an effective system for *systematic* self-development.

With reference to a coherent system, all intended operations are starting with the underlying fundamental idea. Strategically, mission and vision are the direction-giving starting points (cf. Kaplan & Norton, 2004). They define the characteristics of the organisation. Mission and vision must be coherent, too. In terms of longevity and quality, they are the result of a systematically organised initial process. They explain, what the organisation stands for, intends to do, and can achieve →the strategy-giving direction. For a seamless flow of energy, a far-reaching coherence on the level of mission and vision should be expected in times of founding and designing the organisation. The exact knowledge of what an organisation can do and achieve is paramount. The translation into manageable processes requires next-level systematic organisation. The roots for the microsystem have emerged. Such coherence supports those processes, which are then starting the living system. The permanent companion in all the arguments remains the methodological approach for that organisational efforts become effective. This involves a number of deeper thoughts, when we think in terms of a system not as an abstract model of understanding the organisation, but as one in which human beings are controlling those essential switches, which are starting and controlling its operations, including the "main switch" which manages the system's live-giving processes. Those driving managers must know what to do and have both skills and capabilities how to do it; how and where improvements are possible, and in particular, which levers provide effectiveness to develop efficiencies for the cutthroat competitive world which Yuvaraj has studied. Indeed, organisations do learn, but again it is not the abstract form of organisational learning, it is the individuals, who do this by experimental discovery, conscious research, routine, and often enough by trial and error. These processes create knowledge and lead to competence. Competence is essential to not only do things effectively and efficiently, but to improve them ongoing, too. In the end, this means that the system depends fundamentally on the extent and level of available managerial competency to systematically organise these processes. With reference to the coherence of the entire system, this makes one decisive part of it.

Competence enables an organisation, public as private ones. It can analyse what is essential for their own and to some extent the layers of adjacent systems, it can create meaningful operations. Competence delivers an additional layer to improve what Christensen, Anthony and Roth (2004) had in mind, when they defined processes as established ways organisations turn resources into products or services. To refine established organisational processes, it needs the competence to tune the flow of resources in the effort to maximise their generally given scarcity. The part of managing knowledge as contributing factor to enhance competence by an administrative act organises structures which are connecting resources for an advantageous throughput as support for beneficial outcomes. In Sanchez and Heene's (2004, p. 39) words, the result is that "[c]ompetence building creates strategic options; competence leveraging exercises strategic options". Competence is part of Pirsig's statement at the beginning of the discourse, that successful organisational models are copied as long as the knowledge about these exists; i.e., there must be a specific level of competence to do so, and it must be systematically managed for success at the same time. That means that competence adds to the key ingredients which a functioning holistic organisational system needs. As there is no automatised self-development, managed knowledge is essential to design the right connections. The better these are, the more effectiveness the entire system can generate and lead then to efficiencies. The challenge is having and/or developing the necessary knowledge for what defines the most effective connections, and where they can be found. The beforementioned strategic view is a supporting connection map of identification. The rather straightforward causality of interconnected criteria demonstrates again the importance of the per se simple understanding that everything is connected with everything. This time it is not about that simplicity is the opposite of complexity. It is about that straightforward simplicity of thinking in systems allows to structure complexity better.

The management which designs and leads an organisation is supposed to have the right knowledge and skills (cf. Kaplan et al., 2004). This supports the ecosystemic view that an interdependence between living and non-living organisms does exist. Whether the outcome is always beneficial for all organisms, as ecosystem theory suggests, too, seems to be likely more conceptual than real. An operating organisation, whether a company or public service, is built by living beings. They also need the connection to non-living components. Competence and capabilities belong to the latter, they are even non-physical. Despite controversial discussion, both can be seen as resources which are building and improving the endogenous organisational viability and progress within wider exogenous systemic layers. Knowledge forms a driving contributor in the entire equation, which furthers those processes building the system and keeping it alive. The creation of new knowledge enhances options and activities of an organisation inside and outside organisational boundaries. To this adds that being competent in one subject area or function, but not in another one still means being competent; but those skills forming the respective competence or the lack of these are differentiating organisational options. That is a matter of strategic importance as well, because it means that competence is no single or auto-centralising node. I.e., the organisation needs a variety of specialisations which are bundled nodes, and organisational competence centres, the hubs. The requirement is that they constitute a systemic order for channelling processes effectively by finding organised access to existing knowledge in and outside the organisation. This can be seen as the enterprise's nervous system. It delivers systematic order. The nerve centres must be effectively and systematically placed within the organisational structure for that they can send the right impulses for the execution of skilful operations. In addition, the various nerve centres must be interconnected for that their combined effect results in possible and also efficient synergies. The interconnected order contributes to build the organised whole, the web of organisational impulses. This web creates starting points for existing as an own competence-based subsystem, which is an interdependent part of the organisation's main system. Different competences lead to distinctive levels of the organisational existence and to varying endogenous and exogenous dynamics. They act as an instigator which needs that the web is systematically managed for that the energising flow through it is competently organised in itself. All is part of the architectural organisation and influenced by the level of a disciplined systematic order: Returning to Morin (2000) the synthesising conclusion is:

> *Complexity means the inseparability of the different elements, which are constituting the everything. I. e., competence, which systematically connects (the) everything, reduces complexity to become better manageable.*

1.3. Competence-Based System Thinking

Meanwhile, competence has become more than an abstract phenomenon. In a biological setting, an organism must be nourished to remain alive and active. In organisational settings, resources can be interpreted as having the role of maintaining and sustaining operations. They are the "food" to accomplish that operations can happen. If resource access is disrupted for a longer time, the system's main purpose of creating operations must stop. Meadows (2008) paints a simplistic, but informative picture when she explains that operational dynamics depend on stockholding. Stockholding is not only a question of having sufficient resources for matters of producing goods. Having a base of resource flows for building competences, or in Yuvaraj's (2011) differentiation for competences and competencies, is equally important, because organisational dynamics depend on continuous improvements and innovation. However, whether raw materials or competencies, when incoming resources are bigger than outgoing goods, stockholding grows. If it is the other way round, then stockholding reduces. If the same value is incoming as outgoing, then there is a sustainable balance (Meadows, 2008). Too many resources block, too few dry out operations and organisational dynamics are gradually declining. That is as simplistic as it can get, but complexity is not distant. It is found in arranging the viable balance. When it comes to competences, for the organisational, hence the organised system that results in complexity. It is not only about having specific types of competences "on stock" or a certain number of competent staff. As argued, the essential driver of dynamics is having the right competencies at various places of the enterprise in systematically organised form. In addition, the risk of, e.g., depending on just one member of staff holding a decisive key competence poses a risk for the entire system. The loss of such competency may not stop operations but reduce them over the time, and can lead to decline if it cannot be replaced. In an ecosystem, the description is about the viability of its interdependent species. In the microsystem of the organisation, those having an individual key competency are becoming a type of a stem cell. If lost, the system's dynamics are reducing; if not replaced in due time, the risk to become a dying system grows. A next factor and reverse logic are that not having competences allocated systematically means the deployment of the valuable resource of competence to little effect. Combining these thoughts brings the importance of the coherent system back. It then identifies coherence as an essential umbrella, which the system vitally needs to function.

Meadows's example on stockholding, taken as a metaphor, and the non-siloed allocation of competence and competencies at the right nodes of the interconnected enterprise, leads to a further central effect of thinking in systems. Systems can develop best if they are kept in balance. That is a matter of strategic importance. Applying the ITO-strategy (input →throughput →output), an input results in a process-based throughput. The calculated output is at maximised status, if it finds sufficient acceptance. However, such ideal state of balance is most times unlikely and will therefore remain widely imperfect. Too many endogenous and exogenous variables are unlikely maintaining a steady flow. It means that competent system regulation must take place to avoid disadvantageous consequences. A regulating form of system maintenance is essential. Typically, subjective self-regulation does exist, e.g., when seasonal adjustments are made. But a frequent source of failure can be found, when organisational systems disappear because adjustments are made too late, are based on too much bounded rationality, or simply for the reason of oversimplified managerial thinking. The consequence is that on a grey line instead of a level of competence a level of incompetence dominates the organisational system. The system becomes unbalanced through incompetence intoxicating its viability. What this induces is that there can be competence, but that human behaviour can inhibit its systematic and rational application through factors of incompetence, which are disturbing the life-supporting balance.

In the long-term, the equilibrium is of decisive importance. Systems themselves are following the principle that they need two factors: Firstly, a relative balance of incoming and processed resources. Secondly, this balance of resources is depending on systematic processes making effective use of them. The two layers are renewing the fundamental logic of the connection between the living and the non-living species. If both layers are kept in relative equilibrium, the objective of an ecosystem – beneficial outcome – comes into reach. The reverse logic then means that systems are not self- or auto-sustaining. Their individual existence follows the same natural laws, they consume resources to be able to exist, and they function to fulfil their purpose. If knowledge is not effectively fed into the system and the competence to keep it alive is underdeveloped, an organisation will operate in environments of self-instability. The competence-based system needs fuel, two layers again. Firstly, the fuel of knowledge is needed to improve and extend existing competences. This enables the organisation to live within its wider system as an organism in its own right. Secondly, fuel must be added for that managerial capabilities can operate the own system competently. The argument is that the more systemic effectiveness exists in an organisation, the more effects for systematic outputs in form of efficiencies will become possible. This is another argument supporting the need of balance. When we think in systems, in the form of the decisive connection of all living and non-living species, then the reason to separate material resources from capabilities is much less essential. What is of the essence instead, is the right connections, and that they are part of a coherent process which can ongoing translate and also transform effective deployment into efficient operations. This balanced systemic organisation is of highly strategic nature.

1.4. Resources, Capabilities, and the Competence

Systemic thinking recommends that maintaining order and organising connections belongs to managements' prime tasks. With reference to the argumentation before, Whittington, Angwin, Regnér, Johnson and Scholes (2022) support that strategic thinking is about the allocation of resources and capabilities in the interest of viability and competitive advantage (cf. Freiling, 2004). The view on resources and capabilities forms part of a controversial discussion. The question, whether capabilities are a resource or not can be seen in both ways. While this question is strategic itself, more important is that both affect strategic options and the organisational microsystems' radius of activities. In Whittington et al.'s understanding, resources (and capabilities) affect reach and scope of an organisation essentially. Importantly, strategy, as systemic key component, is never distant in both reflection and consideration of thinking in systems. The wide use in the literature is to write about R&C, resources and capabilities. Instead, Whittington et al. extend the differentiation further between competence and capabilities and provide some alternative explanation. This way, they provide a filter. They explain resources and competences as two components of strategic capability. The first, resources, are the assets which organisations have or use. The second, competences, defines how those assets are deployed effectively (Whittington et al., 2022). The differentiating view, which admittedly adds to the confusing taxonomy with reference to what is capability and what competence is then explained in a table, which can be compressed into its key constituents of interest (see table 1.3):

Table 1.3: Key constituents of strategic capabilities

	Strategic capability	
Resources: What the organisation has	Physical | Financial | Human	Competences: What the organisation does well
	Long-term survival and competitive advantage	

For the systems-strategic argumentation, one key conclusion can be drawn: first-order criteria are long-term and survival. In terms of systems, the importance to establish connections between all living (human) and non-living (physical, financial) elements to achieve these key objectives is again, and additionally demonstrated. What the table also expresses, through the close connection of resources and (here) competences, is that perceiving them as a resource or not, is not a one-layered option. This counts equally, if capability is exchanged with competence. The construct is part of a complex and varying understanding, whether competence/capability is separate from resources or not. I.e., whether such differentiation between "what the organisation has" and "what the organisation does well" can be accepted as the defining distinction between distinctions. Whittington et al.'s explanation follows a systematic, i.e., causal logic. However, it is none which is comprehensive enough or justifiable beyond the more simplistic managerial and/or economic purposes, cf. competitive advantages. They remain transitional, i.e., not long-term (Iansiti & Levien, 2004). Yet, the conclusion for systems thinking is that further underlying connections of influence are extracted. They are displaying more details for the practice-oriented understanding of the system's main task, to run forward-leading and system-sustaining operations. I.e., the evidence for the case of a competence-based system gets stronger. The system of competence becomes closely connected to strategy, and quasi, as a side effect, there also is evidence that straightforward simplicity which does not take accompanying complex contexts into consideration cannot be achieved.

With reference to competence, an entirely new dimension with the power of Schumpeter's (1950) Wind of Creative Destruction is actually joining "the" system: Artificial Intelligence. AI will create completely unknown, and in their form unprecedented dimensions: the non-living connection is starting to contribute what the living being did exclusively before. But that is not the end of this development. Barney and Hesterley (2012) refer to Hill and Jones, and to Hitt, Ireland and Hoskisson, when they differentiate that resources are fundamentally financial, physical, individual, and organisational capital attributes. Capabilities instead contribute to the use of these resources for strategic implementation. This exemplarily demonstrates which attempts do exist to come to closer or more differentiating definitions on what are capabilities. The interface between living and non-living organism is already detected: is artificial intelligence which will widely substitute human skills and capabilities then a hybrid? The answer to this question with reference to artificial intelligence will become most interesting. By former definitions it is a non-living organism, also a resource. Very soon, it can be widely, perhaps even fully used for mathematical, rational strategic implementation, and resource allocation of all types. AI will certainly lead to many other fields for which a renewal of the existing theoretical body becomes unavoidable. What is of particular interest is, that the use of artificial intelligence eliminates one essential factor – for the good and the bad: emotion-based erratic human behaviour. That will change systems fundamentally. On the one hand, those weaknesses human behaviour owns will disappear. Correctly programmed and self-, even auto-learning, the right node of competence (or will it then be competency in Yuvaraj's (2011) meaning?) will make decisions entirely rational. Probably in better expression absolutely statistical and emotionless. AI-based non-emotion may follow patterns of strict logic and complete discipline as the future systemic normal. But there are many serious dangers whose extent is as unknown yet, as the many benefits.

The resulting effect may improve the factor competence within systems. The factor of bounded rationality is dismantled from feelings and follows algorithmic methodology. Strict (discipline) rational and analytical thinking (logic) may detect easier (methodology) what is information and what is noise only. In the systemic view, competence is built on bounded rationality, which assumes that decisions are based on imperfect information (Simon, 1957). Simon's view of bounded rationality is "the task … to replace the global rationality of economic man with the kind of rational behaviour that is compatible with the access to information and the computational capacities that are actually possessed by organisms, including man, in the kinds of environments in which such organisms exist" (1955, p. 99). No mistake should be made. It would be short-sighted to reduce both effects and impact on economic man alone. The other side is that the lack of emotions can lead to severe social implications, which can negatively impact on the superior level of the social system. Again, the right balance is likely essential to avoid the pure machine behaviourism of and in the system (cf. Anonymous, 2001). These thoughts are attributing an important facet to what von Bertalanffy wrote in 1968: Systems theory is not a new theory of management; it is a new way of studying and conceptualising organisations. To this Scott adds the four strengths of the design to deal with complexity, the attempt to do so with precision, e. g., AI, to take a holistic view, e.g., Bronfenbrenner's (1979) systems model, and that it is a theory of emergent actions and outcomes at the collective level emerging from the actions and interactions of the individuals that make up the collective (Anonymous, 2001). The essential balance of this construct with socio-economic strands and interfaces needs superior managerial skills of supervision and control, and the knowledge on organising the order for keeping the system alive.

1.5. Is Capability a Resource?

For Whittington et al. (2022) resources and capabilities, and/or competences are creators of promising dynamics. Therefore, the – systemic – question whether capability is now a resource or whether it is something separate, different as much literature suggests, needs further reflection. Often the separation is made between resources as being only all those things a firm can use to produce goods and services, i.e., the meaningful operational organisation of non-living materials, then capabilities are different, non-living and non-physical (Christensen et al., 2004). However, why do human resources exist, then? They are of systemic importance and character. Thinking in systems connects the living with the non-living. The system lives by creating meaningful processes. All what makes resources by the given definition is not starting live-giving processes (input), before capabilities connect (throughput) these resources, for that something meaningful arises (output). The beneficial connectedness is what allows to prosper and survive in a system. The competence-based effective use of the non-living by the living; the strategic development of the organisation by the living for making better outputs differentiates. For the organisational inside-in perspective this means organising the more efficient use of resources for the maximisation of outputs, which creates systematic order and organisation in the effort to reduce scarcity and to optimise the own system's health, and this way its chances for survival. In this understanding, capabilities can be assessed as an essential resource, which owns differences through its human input. Furthermore, based on Christensen et al.'s (2004) view on resources, it can be justified that capabilities building competence can also be assets (keyworkers). Through their competency organisations can buy (hire) or sell (e.g., patents), build (staff training and development), or destroy (fire) when they do not or cannot embed these in the knowledge-base of the firm in a better-informed way. This leads to the assumption that the meaning of everything is connected with everything also adds that living-living, living-non-living, and non-living-non-living interactions should be seen versatile and as essential for systemic dynamics. It is not the strict order of this or that, but the effective composition of all three options. The result is that effectiveness is multi-layered as well.

Revisiting the rather rapid emergence of artificial intelligence builds a further connection and bridge. The living creates an artificial clone of its own strategic thinking, which by algorithms "rationally" decides about the deployment of other non-living resources. (Is it only the deployment of those non-living?) Through self-development – the learning artificial intelligence – the system improves its processes. Based on the high-speed and emotionless decision-making processes, artificial intelligence can reach a state in which it will outperform human thinking. It is not the question of what is today, but what will be in the not distant future. Thinking this scenario through, theoretically non-living resources can be combined to form an own system, which will entirely auto-operate one day. Therefore, the argument is that if such borderlines have existed and, depending on the individual view, may still exist, they are rapidly blurring and by radical innovative thinking they will disappear. The resource may then be called Artificial

Capability. The core principle that everything is connected with everything will then raise the expectation that such system, once established, can autonomously create operations (the system's process-based evidence of existence) without needing permanent human control or even without any such control.

There is no question that this has serious consequences on the level of societies and their development. However, such radical societal re-orientation is not new. This time it may become the most serious challenge which the existing global system has faced. The base of competence will need a new definition because much competence can be substituted much faster. The living-based competence system must expect not to meet but to be confronted with the non-living based competence system. The factor of human behaviour could either become its own big problem or the real advantage. The mechanism of interfaces allowing to control the system, the master switch, may prove to become the most decisive part of thinking in systems. The central question for this discussion becomes, whether the artificial system is a resource, a capability in its own right, but maybe most importantly, which knowledge is needed to manage the resulting complexity. If an artificial and the presently existing capability do coexist, a different two-level game can be predicted.

Synthesising the arguments under the umbrella of an (eco)system's connectedness allows the interpretation, too, that artificial intelligence is building the interface by which a non-living type of specific resource is starting to replace what originally created the living organism's particularity. Consequentially, the operational proximity of human and artificial intelligence blurs now existing borderlines, which, as a consequence, are then becoming more artificial themselves. In addition, such differentiation between resources and capabilities leads to a discussion of even more philosophical nature. What is not changing is that competence-building and running a competence-based system continues to depend on resources and capabilities, whether human or artificial. At least, one of both must supply what was introduced as fuel before. Artificial intelligence is not the first step in this direction, it is probably the first one, which can be attributed to the use of the notion intelligence and the direct comparison of what it, in Morin's (2005) direction of thoughts, auto-develops. The earlier step can be explained by Iansiti and et al. (2004), who have coined the keystone strategy. In this exemplary construct, the typical keystone is not the imitable or non-imitable competence of the living being, it is the non-living Internet. Today, the Internet is the (nearly) omni-connecting point of reference. Strictly speaking it may be debatable whether the Internet is a resource, a product, or a service. Not debatable instead is that the Internet has changed ways, forms, and channels to create and establish connections, and it systemically and systematically changed a myriad of processes and operations. The Internet has transformed the global transactional and interactional ways of economic and social connectedness. It has disaggregated human behaviour and reaggregated both in a now different system. The same question then: Is the Internet resource or, when carefully reading the provided definition on capability, is not there some reason attributing capability to it as well? However, the reference to the Internet as the resource, which is organising and bringing order to daily lives, connects people through, e.g., social media, and creates processes. This qualifies it as a system in its own right, which correctly seen, and strategically is the system's connecting keystone (cf. Iansiti et al., 2004). The point is that the Internet is a non-living, in limited form self-learning and self-developing system, in which the living organisms are being the fuelling part of it. The Internet as driving keystone which starts processes and organises, is driven by third parties. Their living-and non-living nature means adopting a hybrid position. The primary driving force, but all is being driven at the same time. Driving, because of the interaction with and through the Internet; driven, because the Internet has changed human behaviour, but also non-human interactions. And, it continues to do so. Philosophically the question is, whether this is self- or auto-development? The entire connection remains volatile and versatile. The Internet was created by living organisms, is further developed, and maintained by these, but it has also developed a specific form of "own" processes leading to capabilities, which are fuelling competences unknown a few decades ago.

This discussion gains further importance when it extends thinking in systems by the separation of resources from capabilities. The controversial discussion circles around the question of contribution to actions (the operation): material assets or material resources (the non-living) in contrast to what, at least until now, the human being contributes – capabilities, skills, and competence/y. Naturally, a differentiation makes sense. The human being can act, produce, waste, destroy. To some limited extent, this counts equally for other living beings in the natural world using non-living raw materials to build nests, open nuts, etc. I e., there exists a systemic difference in form of the user and the used thing, but both are connected for the system's viability. At the beginning of the discussion, ecosystem theory concluded that the connection between living beings and the non-living species in a system is interactional and interdependent. Everything is connected *to* everything and *with* everything. In systems thinking that can be condensed to the view that there is one differentiation of importance: Once more, and that in strategic terms, too, the creativity to shape, design, organise, and alter is a core factor signifying the living. The non-living supports and delivers for that these processes can be materialised. On the other hand, nature's non-living beings can create as well, e.g., when two chemical resources meet and combine, they trigger a reaction. The difference is that human creativity and curiosity owns the ability to make such encounter not random but planned. It can add the factor of organised repetition. Such organised process of "operations" can further be seen as systematics. Research laboratories are one example for a centre of organised discoveries, whose results may change the existing system and its status quo. They can even be the birthplace of a new system. It means that creativity and curiosity are organising such encounters for specific purposes. We can also say that there is a certain systematic to manage these resources for best possible use and outcome. As soon as this is finding a stable and productive outcome which achieves acceptance in form of at least sufficient returns, effectiveness has been reached and then allows to improve processes for more efficiencies. More capabilities start to develop better organised processes by finding new applications, improvements, recipes, which are both strengthening the existing base of competence and are leading to new capabilities, but also knowledge. The option to start the development cycle of new competences emerges in addition.

1.6. The View on Information and Knowledge

For a meaningful analysis, attention is drawn to Lindgren and Rasmussen's (2003) work. They "argue that there is a misfit between existing competence systems handling formalised competence descriptions related to well-defined tasks and the dynamic nature of knowledge work. Knowledge-based organisations distinguished by changing conditions, unforeseen requirements, continuous learning, and a constant need for innovation require competence systems based on a richer interpretation of competence" (Lindgren et al., 2003, p. 19). Meadows holds that "[m]any of the interconnections in systems operate through the flow of information. Information holds systems together and plays a great role in determining how they operate" (2008, p. 14). Firstly, it confirms, that despite given limitations of information, which are subject to bounded rationality, information remains key. That is understandable, because information enables decision-makers to rationally analyse (methodology), how resources can be used best (disciplined use) →their strategic implementation (logic). Secondly, to the conceptual outline of the organisation as the non-living holder of the main system, information adds supporting input for competence-systemic processes. It is not difficult to understand that competence-based systems (discipline as instruction) are supporting to strengthen competence (organisational logic) by incoming information and by processing information (relying on and related to methodology). In system-theoretical understanding this attributes to competence the role of a support system, which adopts several forms and shapes. Lindgren et al. (2013) hold that these are based on a rationalistic view on competence. The thought on competence having rationalistic thinking as foundation is generally essential. However, what becomes emphasised is that a line of coherence of these interrelated systems can be drawn. The more and better they are connected, the more and better systemic life-giving energy can flow and send the necessary impulses through the entire system. This only reads like simple causality. In reality it is opposed by the enormous complexity of organising such flow best possibly through seamless channels. It is and remains a matter of systematic management being necessary to not only organise such coherence, it is of equal importance to make sure that it remains so (cf. Morin's notion of the self, not auto maintenance).

What remains central in these reflections is the permanent need for information. The system needs information to know and learn, how to operate and how to develop further. I.e., operations of the system are depending on the processed flow of information and equally on their quality. If the flow of information stops, there are two options left: Continue operations in the best belief of what was known before (discipline). This makes it an assumption or an informed guess but bears the risk to become a waste of resources. The other option is to stop all operations in the hope that the flow will restart soon. That avoids the possible waste of resources but affects the output. If the flow of information remains incomplete or disrupted, the system's viability becomes endangered. The other need is the quality of information which means that the message which is delivered provides sufficient validity and reliability (methodology) for that the system can produce the right output (logic). That means for the sender comprehensiveness and completeness of the messages, and for the receiver the right interpretation of the information provided. Simplistic, consequential, and easily understandable, effectiveness-oriented. What makes it complex is that knowledge-building and competence-building are interdependently linked to both the flow and the quality of information. As Meadows confirms, missing information is one of the most common reasons causing system malfunction. In the discussion on systemic competence, information adopts the key function of being the bonding element. Skills, capabilities, competence, and knowledge are individually and mutually depending on information, its analysis, translation into resource allocation, and the organisation of the flow of processes. The entire competence-base is tightly connected with the main system and other organisational subsystems by exactly the continuity of the exchange of information. This also means that information must contribute to maintain the coherence of the entire system, internally and externally. The causal-logic conclusion is that the prerequisite for such achievement is that the flow of information must be organised systematically.

The argumentation returns to and highlights that systematics and coherence are bonding components for keeping the main system alive and in balance. Their strategic presence protects systems' health and functionality to continuously produce meaningful operations. This conclusion adds further importance to the often-neglected fact that effectiveness comes before any efficiency. The fundamental need for effectiveness depends on rational thinking in structures of causal logic. Thinking, which, despite bounded rationality, influences the quality of informed processes and is based on rational behaviour (Simon, 1957). Rational behaviour links to games theory. As one prerequisite, it supposes that participants in a game are acting rationally (Heifetz, 2012). The reduction of rationality weakens systems because typically methodological objectivity ≠ the subjectivity of assumptions and beliefs. The discussion's objective is creating the understanding that despite more and more systems' complexities are explored and discussed, there is the permanent return to the very same elements making systems. I.e., the assumption that hyper-complexity exists everywhere and grows further, is countered by a rather narrow nucleus of those elements involved, or those dimensions to which these elements can be attributed. Rationality, effectiveness, linear and non-linear actions, or information, they all belong to those cells, which are making systems, but the core of all, which has continuously developed, is the umbrella-concept of (inter)connectedness. The often passively existing culture of organisational silos must then be considered as active reduction of effectiveness. Even if every silo is based on a high level of available competencies, the lack or avoidance of connections reduces the system's effectiveness as a whole. Silos are reducing the flow and are filtering information. This affects the firm's competence base negatively and endangers the viability of the entire system. It was Scott Poole's (Anonymous, 2001) view that the holistic perspective is one of the four strengths. We can suppose that the different emphasis, dose, and combination of these enterprise-chemical elements, which are shaping the direction of the system and the outputs, which it produces, are holding the key to maximisation of outcomes and reduction of waste. It then offers ways to develop the competence-based organisation as a loop of permanent self-development and improvement.

1.7. Competence as a System

This headline also intends being a question which needs an answer. The danger regarding the general openness of systems theory is that it seems to invite to easily declare a phenomenon to be a system. As von Bertalanffy (1969) has stated, systems have not only reached various fields of science, but also entered popular thinking and jargon. Consequentially, it would be a simplistic understanding to think that every phenomenon is a system. It is always important to carefully separate popular perception from scientific, hence defendable study and critical reflection. In the theory's understanding a system is made of and must meet a number of defining criteria for that it can be understood as a system in its own right. If the reader wants to follow Luhmann, then the synthesised form which he adopts from Parsons (cited in Luhmann, 2016) is the assumption that components do exist, whose combination make actions possible. As Luhmann continues, it is the identification of components and the design of an analytic theory of action on their basis. The result then is Parsons's analytic realism. What I already did at the beginning was to identify the required components in form of ability, skill, capability, and knowledge which are supposed – the above theory of action here – to design the competence-base of an organisation. That means that systems theory advantageously furthers the design or creation of a system by organising a variety of components accordingly for that they can (inter)act as intended. It means that they are starting live-giving processes for the system in a narrower and also wider understanding of what makes operative action possible. When it comes to designing a functioning system, then two factors are of the essence: Firstly, how can those identified components be systemically organised to achieve the intended outcome? Naturally, many, if not most things can be organised in one way or another, but not every design or underlying process must necessarily start an operation. Hence, systemic organisation, the analytical part, means to bring things, e.g., resources, into a meaningful order for that a system's key criterion, processes leading to operations, can be constituted. Next then, how can they be connected best possibly, the matter of systematic effectiveness? It is a core interest for maximising the outcome. It cannot be a simplistic connection of drawing lines from element or systemic organism 1 to element/organism 2, and so on. Effectiveness of the system signifies that connections are made to deliver something useful and outcome-oriented for that the system itself is viable within its environment. E.g., connecting electrical components in the effort to produce a radio is one side of the coin. Per se that meets one prerequisite. As well, decisive is having the right connections for that no short circuit occurs. That also means the output must operate as a radio, i.e., delivering exactly what an output is supposed to do. If it does, it would create a manufacturing microsystem of simplistic importance for the operations of a radio-manufacturer. Simplistic because the question is, is the system, which the organisation builds, still viable? Can it be meaningful in times, when radios are not in demand anymore? I.e., can this operational microsystem and its superior level of the organisation survive in an environment whose demand for radios has disappeared? The answer to this question connects the two essential layers of "meaningful" and "viable".

The starting point for designing a system which is based on competence can be found in two essential nodes, which are forming their own meaningful connection. For an economic organisation and/or public service, e.g., that is strategy and market-orientation. Their processes are supporting mission and vision for that an input of resources results in viable outputs by the use of an advantageously organised throughput. Returning to the ITO-strategy, the architecture of the process can be understood as circular effectiveness. The system becomes successful when it delivers a viability-supporting return. The many different layers of competences and/or competencies, which it needs are evident. The organisational process stands on two pillars of a priori categories: Firstly, to deliver a functioning product or service, and significantly more importantly, to deliver ones, whose market acceptance supports the organisation's viability in return. This way, ability, skill, capability, and knowledge do not only need an effective form of organisation, which is strategically analysis-based, it also needs efficiencies for the improvement of viability. The organised structures in their holistic architecture depend on meaningful connections. They are relying on the organisation's collective competence connected in the competence-based system. It supports both start and continuation of worthwhile processes to keep alive what interacts as, and equally makes a systemic architecture.

What this explains is that the competence of an organisation is no fixed virtue; it has a variety of options with consequentially underlying threats and opportunities. The core point of thinking in systems and their management may then be found in acting agents' knowledge that competence is strongly connected with strategic direction. This view is critically seen by Witzel (2009), Pirsig (cited in Meadows, 2008). Both can be supported by own long-term ethnographic research: the organisational world shows little such knowledge and struggles with strategic understanding. Despite such existing weaknesses, which can explain a good number of organisational weaknesses in performance, two causal factors of importance are:

1. *Strategy influences the decision which competence-base the organisation needs to build and extend;*
2. *Existing competences decide, which strategy the organisation can advantageously adopt, and which are out of reach and scope* (cf. Whittington et al., 2022).

That is neither a static decision being valid forever, nor is it a decision being in the uninfluenced autonomy of the organisation. The organisation is and remains part of its ecosystem or at least system in which it navigates. External influences and turbulences are permanently challenging and demand to be respected in all decision-making processes. This reduction of autonomy reduces choice and control, which the organisation can exert over its strategy. This influences the resource allocation, which then continues to impact on possible outputs. The domino effect is evident – everything is connected with everything. The result comes as another aspect of ongoing imperfectness, even if the level of competence is high and difficult to imitate. The overarching systemic order is subject to what Peter Drucker once formulated as the permanent struggle for survival. Systems of all kind or sizes, they emerge and disappear; competence is built and becomes irrelevant, if not strategically, systematically, and timely renewed. Coherence of the system means that not only the internal coherence is of importance, it needs to be equally coherently aligned with the external system. This counts for all types of organisations equally.

1.8. Conclusion: Everything Is Connected with Everything

The value of the organisational competence-based system relies and depends on effective architectural structures administering the collective of available competences in seamless flows of value-adding information. The energising flow is based on distinctive and multiple dimensions of agents' individual competencies (cf. Yuvaraj, 2011). Competence is made of the applied side of capabilities and the reflective and/or theory-informed side of knowledge. Both are especially valuable when they are cross-functional or cross-disciplinary, i.e., non-silo and non-monolithic. The main system connects the organisation's living and non-living organisms for that the competence-based flow of capabilities produces an output. The ability to translate competences builds capabilities. They are forming nodes for systematically organised processes. Their output supports the system's viability and an effectively managed return moves up to improve and/or extend the competence base in return. It is a simple, because causally-consequential circular structure. This way, it is effective, nevertheless complex to achieve. The resulting value depends on the organisation's culture and knowledge-based management to organise a systemic cross-functional flow of information. To achieve this requires multiple mechanisms to secure that knowledge and information is stored and made available. The cycle organises meaningful connections in a process of permanent flow which has the power to trigger and sustain the system's operations. It is not difficult to see that this is equally part of a systematic management and a significant contribution to build effectiveness.

Step-by-step I have not only argued that it is justifiable to consider competence as a system, more implicitly, I developed a three-dimensional artefact, convinced that systems are a natural artefact of organisation, and also that nature must be based on triangles (cf. Fuller cited in Keidel, 2010).

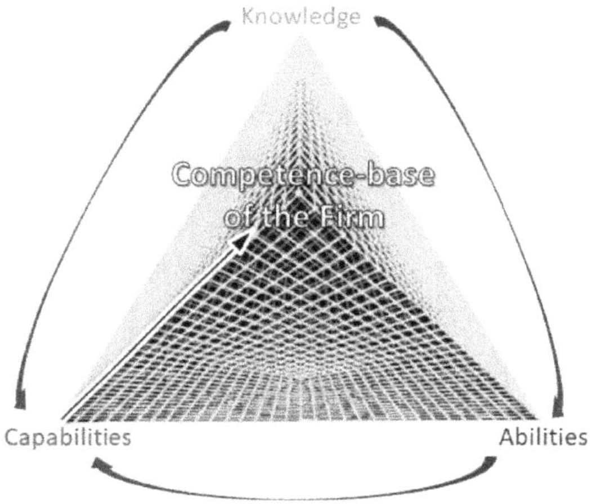

Figure 1.1: Interconnected and interdependent – everything must be connected with everything (own graph)

References

Akiyama, E. & Kaneko, K. (2000). Dynamical Systems Game Theory and Dynamics of Games. *Physica D*, 147 (2000), pp. 221–258.

Anonymous. (2001). *Systems Theory*. Lexington, KY: University of Kentucky. http://www.uky.edu/~drlane/orgcomm/325ch04.ppt

Balogun, J., Hope Hailey, V. & Viardot, E. (2005). *Stratégies du Changement* (2nd ed.). Paris: Pearson Education France.

Barney, J. B. & Hesterley, W. S. (2012). *Strategic Management and Competitive Advantage: Concepts* (4th ed.). Upper Saddle River, NJ: Pearson Education, Inc.

Bronfenbrenner, U. (1979). *The Ecology of Human Development: Experiments by Nature and Design*. Cambridge, MA: Harvard University Press.

Campbell, N. A., Reece, J. B., Taylor, M. R., Simon, E. J. & Dickey, J. L. (2008). *Biology: Concepts and Connections with Mybiology* (6th ed.). San Francisco, CA: Benjamin Cummins.

Christensen, C. M., Anthony, S. D. & Roth, E. A. (2004). *Seeing What's Next: Using the Theories of Innovation to Predict Industry Change*. Boston, MA: Harvard Business School Press.

Cox III, J. F. & Schleier, J. G. (Eds.). (2010). *Theory of Constraints Handbook*. New York, NY: McGraw-Hill.

Freiling, J. (2004). A Competence-Based Theory of the Firm. *Management Revue*, 15 (1), pp. 27–52.

Heifetz, A. (2012). *Game Theory: Interactive Strategies in Economics and Management*. Cambridge: Cambridge University Press.

Iansiti, M. & Levien, R. (2004). *The Keystone Advantage: What the New Dynamics of Business Ecosystems Mean for Strategy Innovation and Sustainability*. Boston, MA: Harvard Business School Press.

Kaplan. R. S. & Norton, D. P. (2004). *Strategy Maps: Converting Intangible Assets into Tangible Outcomes*. Boston, MA: Harvard Business Press.

Keidel, R. W. (2010). *The Geometry of Strategy: Concepts for Strategic Management*. Abingdon: Routledge.

Leonhard, D. & Sensiper, S. (1998). The Role of Tacit Knowledge in Group Innovation. *California Management Review*, 40 (3), pp. 112–132.

Lindgren, P. & Rasmussen, O. H. (2013). The Business Model Cube. *Journal of Multi Business Model Innovation and Technology*. Aalborg University, pp. 135–182.

Lindgren, R., Stenmark, D. & Ljungberg, J. (2003). Rethinking Competence Systems for Knowledge-Based Organizations. *European Journal of Information Systems*, 2003 (12), pp. 18–29.

Luhmann, N. (2016). *Introduction to Systems Theory*. Cambridge: Polity Press.

Meadows, D. H. (2008). *Thinking in Systems: A Primer*. White River Junction, VT: Chelsea Green Publishing.

Moore, J. F. (1993). Predators and Prey: A New Ecology of Competition. *Harvard Business Review*, May/June 1993.

Morin, E. (2000). *Les sept savoirs nécessaires à l'éducation du futur*. Paris: Editions du Seuil.

Morin, E. (2005). *Introduction à la pensée complexe*. Paris: Editions du Seuil.

Odum, E. P. (1971). *Fundamentals of Ecology*. 3rd ed. New York, NY: Saunders.

Sanchez, R. & Heene, A. (2004). *The New Strategic Management: Organization, Competition, and Competence*. New York, NY: John Wiley & Sons.

Schumpeter, J. A. (1950). *Capitalism, Socialism and Democracy* (3rd ed.). New York: Harper & Row.

Simon, H. A. (1955). A Behavioral Model of Rational Choice. *Quarterly Journa* *of Economics*, 69 (1), pp. 99–118.

Simon, H. A. (1957). *Models of Man*. New York, NY: John Wiley.

Su, Z., Peng, M. W. & Xie, E. (2015). A Strategy Tripod Perspective on Knowledg Creation Capability. *British Journal of Management*, 00, pp. 1–19.

Todeva, E. (2007). *Behavioural Theory of the Firm*. Munich: Personal RePE Archive. https://mpra.ub.uni-muenchen.de/52841/1/MPRA_paper_52841

Vakola, M., Soderquist, K. E. & Prastacos, G. P. (2007). *International Journal o* *Manpower*, 28 (3/4), pp. 260–275.

Von Bertalanffy, L. (1969). *General System Theory: Foundations, Development* *Applications* New York, NY: George Braziller.

Whittington, R., Angwin, D., Regnér, P., Johnson, G. & Scholes K. (2022) *Exploring Strategy* (13th ed.). Harlow: Pearson Education Ltd.

Witzel, M. (2009). *Management History: Text and Cases*. Abingdon: Routledge.

Yuvaraj, R. (2011). Competency Mapping: A Drive for Indian Industries *International Journal of Scientific & Engineering Research*, 2 (8), pp. 1–7.

Marie Sitter and Patrick Szillat

2. Corporate Social Responsibility Authenticity and Its Impact on Consumer Behaviour – A Multiple Regression Analysis as a Contribution to Innovation Management

Abstract: Corporate Social Responsibility (CSR) activities have become essential to corporate competitiveness, especially in the fashion industry. This study proposes a conceptual model on the influence of the CSR attributes consistency, fit, and impact on consumer perceived CSR authenticity as well as brand attitude in a quantitative research approach. The statistical analysis of the study's online survey proves a positive effect of CSR attributes on consumer perceived CSR authenticity and shows indication of the mediating role of CSR authenticity on the relation between CSR attributes and brand attitude. The findings of this study enrich the current knowledge of empirical research on authenticity and CSR. The study contributes to the development of an interdisciplinary theory of authenticity and practical recommendations for CSR strategies as well as to the field of innovation management.

Keywords: CSR, fashion industry, competitiveness, brand attitude, strategic management

2.1. Introduction

In 1962 Friedman stated that following the interest of shareholders, referring to profit maximisation, is supposed to be the highest goal of a business. This view is long outdated because nowadays, companies also have to consider the interests of other stakeholder groups and need to follow socially responsible practices (Fatma & Rahman, 2016). An organisation's voluntary commitment to achieve and implement social, environmental, consumer and human rights goals into its strategy and operations is defined by corporate social responsibility (CSR) (European Commission, 2001). In the framework of continuous innovation management, CSR has become an inevitable part of business ethics and strategy since stakeholder expectations have grown incredibly high in the last decades (Scherer & Palazzo, 2011). Simultaneously the demand from stakeholders for more sustainable businesses is growing (Du et al., 2007, 2015; Kim & Lee, 2019). Consumers feel increasingly impacted by societal issues such as climate change, racial or Gender inequality (Yeomans, 2018) and want brands to solve the problems created by society (Edelman, 2022).

The last decades were driven by the ever more efficient mass production and the hunt for the cheapest and fastest way of satisfying consumers – a new business model, "fast fashion", developed in the fashion industry (Bhardwaj & Fairhurst, 2010). Designing collections quick and trendy to produce cheaply and sell at low prices was perfected. Contrary to this, newer studies proved that consumers are willing to pay more if a company engages in CSR activities (Fatma & Rahman, 2016). Corporate social responsibility (CSR) activities – also in the context of innovation management – have become essential to corporate competitiveness (Porter & Kramer, 2007; Porter & Kramer, 2011), especially in the fashion industry. Nowadays, fast fashion brands like H&M, Zara, and Uniqlo have rethought their activities and developed new strategies to follow the new motions in society since stakeholders are developing their claims (Choi et al., 2019).

In addition to the practical developments, the scientific examination in the field of CSR is rapidly increasing and maturing (Ji et al., 2022). In a summative study by Song and Dong (2022) it was concluded that a lack of investigation of the underlying mechanisms of CSR and its outcomes causes major gaps in the theorisation (Wang et al., 2020). In practice, this scientific gap indicates that the decisions and actions of a company or institution cannot be made with sufficient theoretical background.

So far, the research field aims to understand the success of CSR activities and factors influencing consumers' perceptions (Alhouti & D'Souza, 2018; Fatma & Rahman, 2016; Mulaessa & Wang, 2017). Literature managed to identify the authenticity of CSR engagement as a critical factor in the construct (Afzali & Kim, 2021; Fatma & Khan, 2022; Jose et al., 2018; Liu & Jung, 2021; Mazutis & Slawinski, 2015). Authenticity in CSR describes the potential of how CSR can create value for the company, stakeholders, and society (Song & Dong, 2022). In combination with the previously mentioned growing scepticism from a consumer's point of view and the development of the fashion industry (Bhardwaj & Fairhurst, 2010), researching CSR in this context is beneficial.

This research aims to explore how consumers perceive the authenticity of CSR activities, specifically in the fast fashion industry, and how this perception is affected by different attributes of a CSR action. In particular, consistency, fit and impact of a CSR activity are explored regarding their positive influence on the perception of CSR authenticity from a consumer's point of view. This is the first hypothesis of the research model. The second hypothesis of the research addresses the mediating role of CSR Authenticity on a consumer's attitude toward a brand. These hypotheses are intended to shed light on the research questions surrounding customer perceptions:

- When surveyed, who responds to this subject and what is the structure of the respondents (age, gender, ethnicity, current residence)?
- Do the selected attributes of CSR activities influence the authenticity of CSR that a consumer perceives positively?
- Does the CSR authenticity perception of a consumer mediate the consumer's attitude toward a brand?

Thus, this study contributes to further theoretical insights on the way to the development of a general theoretical concept. In addition, this study's results contribute to scientifically substantiating practical decisions of companies on the design of CSR activities and creating a better understanding of the consumer perspective. Considering the challenge in the field of CSR, this is especially relevant in the fashion industry, particularly in fast fashion.

2.2. Literature Review

2.2.1. CSR and CSR Activities

It is essential to state definitions in research for the term CSR since different approaches are being used. This study suggests that CSR is a voluntary activity by companies with "the inclusion of social and environmental concerns in their business operations and interaction with stakeholders" (Van Marrewijk, 2003, p. 102). Other studies' definitions go a step further and state the CSR engagement of a company as an umbrella term that includes every environmental, social and philanthropic issue that a firm reacts to by changing its beliefs and work structures (McEwen, 2004; Sampaio et al., 2012). In the early work of Carroll (1979), another frequently used conceptual model explained an approach to CSR in a corporate performance context. According to the model, it is not sufficient for a strategic CSR Activity to create a virtuous circle between social contributions and economic performance through the efficient use of limited resources. A newer and often accepted description is from Carroll (2016, p. 2) pyramid of CSR, stating it as "the economic, legal, ethical, and discretionary expectations that society has of organisations at a given point in time" involving an outside view on a company.

While issues such as environmental protection and social justice in companies were more of a stand-alone feature of a brand a few years ago, they became indispensable in any good organisation. It is time for companies to adapt strategies, create solutions for ongoing changes (Du et al., 2015), and implement CSR into day-to-day business operations (Rodriguez-Gomez et al., 2020). Shareholders expect CSR to be firmly integrated into corporate strategy (Bhardwaj, 2016;

Kirchoff et al., 2016; Nardella et al., 2020). Implementing sustainability strategies is needed to make companies more competitive (Du et al., 2015; Jalilvand et al., 2017). Furthermore, organisations with good sustainability ratings performed significantly better than those with poor ratings (Khan et al., 2016). Studies also show that the perception of CSR positively influences customer behaviour (Fatma & Rahman, 2016; Mohr & Webb, 2005), such as loyalty or brand relationship quality (Cha et al., 2016; Jarvis et al., 2017; Lo, 2020).

Literature shows that a company's CSR effort is associated with a competitive advantage (Vilanova et al., 2009). In particular, Porter and Kramer (2007, 2011) argue that companies should align their CSR activities with corporate strategy. Moreover, CSR Activities should only address social and environmental issues that impact society significantly and the company's bottom line simultaneously. After 1990, studies started focussing on the consumer point of view to understand how CSR affects consumers' outcomes, which can be necessary for a company's image. The interest of consumers in CSR activities is increasing at the same time (Sen & Bhattacharya, 2001). Research shows that CSR activities influence consumers' evaluation of a company and behavioural outcomes such as recommendation intention, the attitude towards the brand (Ellen et al., 2006) or the purchase intent (Groza et al., 2011). Consumers are even willing to pay more to companies that engage in CSR (Fatma & Rahman, 2016). These observations lead companies to use CSR engagement as an instrument to attract and retain customers because it might influence responses and consumers' perceptions of CSR activities. Consumers' interest in CSR activities has increased rapidly in the last decades (Fatma & Khan, 2022). The combination of these trends raises new research questions in the framework of growing scepticism of consumers and many different CSR approaches of companies. One of the most important aspects of CSR research is the consideration of the performance-determining characteristics of CSR Activities (Yoo & Lee, 2018).

2.2.2. Authenticity

2.2.2.1. Theoretical Framework

In recent literature, perceptions of authenticity appear closely related to perceptions of truth (Grayson & Martinec, 2004; Morhart et al., 2015). In this respect, it is essential to understand what is perceived as true in authenticity. According to (Moulard et al., 2021), the three types of truth are true-to-ideal, true-to-fact and true-to-self. All three types of truth usually occur together, albeit to different degrees. However, although all three types of truth are mentioned in the authenticity literature and research, most empirical studies focus on the ideal-to-self type of truth. The study also assesses the ideal-to-self type of truth. CSR activities are predominantly based on values and adherence through socio-political engagement rather than on facts.

The study of perception is the goal of cognitive psychology and socio-psychology, with the question of how information is processed in people's minds. Bayesian models of cognition (Perfors et al., 2011) assume that in the marketing context, consumers' assessments of the Impact of brand activities influence their perception of the brand's authenticity. This information tells consumers how much the activities match their expectations – or ideals – and how much the CSR activism matches the brand's values (Brashier & Marsh, 2020). Social psychological attribution theory (Heider, 1946) explains how people attribute causes to behaviour, which also reflects the understanding of self-perception (Moulard et al., 2021). When a company undertakes a CSR activity, it may do so either for internal reasons, such as its values or external reasons, such as pressure from stakeholders and competitors (Moulard et al., 2021). Consumers will perceive CSR activities as more authentic if they attribute the behaviour to internal reasons of a value-based agenda. In this respect, the attributed voluntary nature of CSR activities is highly important for the perception of authenticity and the source of information for the attribution of consumers' perceptions Kelley (1973).

2.2.2.2. *CSR Authenticity*

Generally, attributes such as genuineness, trustfulness, credibility, and actuality are positively connected to the term authenticity (Alhouti et al., 2016; Chiu et al., 2012). If a company is genuinely responsible and engaged in CSR, authenticity is defined as the stakeholders' opinion about the reliability, sincerity, and authenticity of an organisation's Activities (Alhouti et al., 2016; Kovács, 2019). Specifically in CSR research, the term authenticity is defined as "the perception of a company's CSR actions as a genuine and true expression of the company's beliefs and behaviour toward a society that extends beyond legal requirements" (Alhouti et al., 2016, p. 1243). Authenticity is interpreted as the alignment of CSR actions with the company's core values, lowering consumer scepticism towards CSR engagement and making them appear genuine (Beckman et al., 2009; Mazutis & Slawinski, 2015; Pérez, 2019). Others state that the alignment between a company's advertisements and the corporate culture's image is perceived as authentic from employees' points of view (Schaefer et al., 2019). So far, studies on CSR Authenticity approach the issue conceptually (Driver, 2006; Mazutis & Slawinski, 2015), while many others use qualitative methods to understand employee perceptions from an organisational perspective (Beckman et al., 2009; Mcshane & Cunningham, 2012). With exploratory research approaches, criteria of authenticity in institutional and social contexts were investigated by Beckman, Colwell and Cunningham (2009). In the last years, the number of empirically researched papers increased and quantified the influencing factors, predictors and outcomes of CSR Authenticity (Pérez, 2019).

As early as 1995, Price, Arnould and Tierney (1995) argued that Authenticity comes from genuine concern for others rather than social responsibility. Other studies discovered that CSR activities are judged authentic when they are perceived as purely socially motivated, which, in turn, leads to a positive reaction towards the company and the act itself (Ellen et al., 2006; Sen et al., 2006). If a company communicates its sincerity about a CSR activity to consumers and the activity genuinely brings solutions to a social or environmental problem, then authenticity can be generated (Foreh & Grier, 2003; Williams, 2014). Alhouti, Johnson and Holloway (2016) suggest that consumers are often sceptical about an organisation's statements about CSR, implicating authenticity influences important consumer decisions.

Beckman, Colwell and Cunningham (2009) describe the importance of authenticity for successfully implementing CSR Activities since authenticity positively impacts the overall consumer perception. Authenticity has increasingly become the focus of modern marketing and communications management studies and practices as the public interest for organisations to be open, honest and genuine is growing (Pérez, 2019). Pérez (2019, p. 334) states that consumers' belief that CSR claims are authentic improves "source credibility by reducing consumer scepticism and enhancing their attributions of corporate expertise and trustworthiness". Indirectly, an authentic CSR message can increase consumers' buying, loyalty and advocacy behaviour (Pérez, 2019). Inauthentic consumer evaluations can lead to the loss of the reputation of companies (Losada-Otálora & Alkire (née Nasr), 2019; Skilton & Purdy, 2017). Due to the importance of authenticity for the perception of CSR activities, research on perceived authenticity and its construct has become a new important subject. Current literature in this field is only slowly building a knowledge base around perceived authenticity's influence on CSR engagement and company attitudes (Alhouti et al., 2016; Moehl & Friedman, 2022).

However, with the new efforts and positive developments for our planet, brands started to invent strategies such as "greenwashing" to appear well-doing (Laufer, 2003). Consumers feel that some brands only act sustainably for profit rather than genuine concern about the world (Drumwright, 1996; Foreh & Grier, 2003; Wagner et al., 2009). Logically, this results in growing consumer scepticism and mistrust about the motives and intentions of CSR activities (Yoo & Lee, 2018). Other studies underlined how critical authenticity in today's world is since modern society developed a widespread lack of trust (Brown et al., 2003; Edelman, 2022; Joo et al., 2019).

A recent study delves deeper into the concept of authenticity and goes beyond a company's core values. According to Afzali and Kim (2021), the congruence of internal motivation for CSR activities in a company and external behaviour leads to the consumer's perception of authentic CSR policies. Joo, Miller and Fink (2019) imply that public serving motives of a CSR activity would show that a company is engaged in CSR because they believe this would be the right thing to do. This study is a very recent research questioning how consumers perceive the authenticity of CSR and which factors influence these consumer perceptions. While it is now known that perceived CSR authenticity impacts a brand's credibility and a consumer's purchasing behaviour, little is known about how consumers judge the authenticity of CSR (Moehl & Friedman, 2022). The question is which attributes of a CSR activity or factors influence the consumer perception of CSR authenticity. It has already been recognised that a company with a long history of CSR engagement will be perceived as more authentic when compared to recent CSR initiatives (Morhart et al., 2015). Still, previous studies have not paid enough attention to CSR authenticity yet, and there is a lack of empirical research investigating why consumers perceive a CSR action as authentic (Fatma & Khan, 2022). It is vital to examine better how authenticity is formed and perceived to understand the factors by which consumers evaluate CSR Authenticity (Fatma & Khan, 2022).

2.2.3. CSR Attributes

Due to the increasing consumer scepticism towards CSR activities, researchers are looking into the factors affecting consumers' perception of CSR activities. CSR attributes are factors associated with a CSR Activity and can positively influence the authenticity of CSR (Latif et al., 2022; Liu & Jung, 2021; Yoo & Lee, 2018).

The study of Beckman, Colwell and Cunningham (2009), for instance, derives seven variables that influence the perception of CSR authenticity, including motivation, impact, relevance, transparency, consistency, and commitment to CSR activities. Other studies identify more dimensions that influence a brand's effort in CSR. For instance, the sustainability of a CSR Activity can have a positive impact(Ellen et al., 2006; Park et al., 2014). Also, consistency, meaning how long the company is actively engaged in one topic, is a factor in the effectiveness of a

CSR Activity (Gupta & Pirsch, 2006; Yoo & Lee, 2018). Further factors identified so far are fit embeddedness (Mcshane & Cunningham, 2012), durability (Kim et al., 2018; Ranfagni & Guercini, 2016), the distinctiveness of CSR (Mazutis & Slawinski, 2015) and perception of motives (Becker-Olsen et al., 2006; Schaefer & Pettijohn, 2006; Yoo & Lee, 2018). The fit of a CSR Activity is part of many critical studies, showing that a CSR activity close to the company's actions and business is a crucial factor for the effectiveness of a CSR action (Alhouti et al. 2016; Gupta & Pirsch, 2006; Sen & Bhattacharya, 2001).

The consideration of consistency in CSR engagement is part of the research of Yoo and Lee (2018) and Joo, Miller and Fink (2019). They also study the fit of a CSR activity as an attribute, which also plays a role in Alhouti, Johnson and Holloway (2016) and (Kim & Lee, 2019). Fatma and Khan (2022) integrate fit (congruence) into their concept and expand it with the influence of a CSR activity. Based on these studies from the last few years, it has become clear that the attributes of consistency, fit and impact of CSR activities are critical. The combination of these attributes of CSR is currently being explored by Liu and Jung (2021), are used as typical characteristics of CSR activities and recommended for further investigation in empirical studies. Therefore, this study will assess the influence of CSR activities' authenticity using this combination.

2.2.4. CSR Consistency

In the context of CSR, consistency is a factor that determines whether a particular behaviour or action takes place continuously from beginning to end. The consistency of CSR Activities in this study refers to the company's overall strategy and its continuous consideration of CSR, meaning invested resources and time consistently go hand in hand with the corporate strategy (L'Etang, 1994). This condition is necessary to maintain a positive impact in experimental research, as it only exists if the customer can recognise this consistency (Ellen et al., 2006).

Previously often cited and further developed studies considered the consistency of CSR engagement of CSR as an essential antecedent (Alhouti et al., 016; Beckman et al., 2009). Park, Lee and Kim (2014) argue that factors like the sustainability of CSR, meaning how consistent CSR activities are performed, need to be studied to understand the effectiveness of CSR activities. As already explored by Beckman, Colwell and Cunningham (2009), further studies say that CSR activities' consistency is highly relevant in studying CSR authenticity and consumer perception (Yoo & Lee, 2018). Morhart et al. (2015) describe a positive effect on the perception of authenticity if the company's CSR engagement has a long history compared to more recent CSR activities.

2.2.5. CSR Fit

A major research topic in the context of CSR research is the fit of CSR (Becker-Olsen et al., 2006; Lii & Lee, 2012; Schaefer & Pettijohn, 2006; Yoo & Lee, 2018), meaning similarities between a company's core products or services and the activity (Menon & Kahn, 2003). This implements CSR fit is defined as congruence between CSR activities and core business activities (Becker-Olsen et al., ; Kernis & Goldman, 2006; Mazutis & Slawinski, 2015). More explicitly expressed by Ellen, Webb and Mohr (2006), CSR fit is a recognised link among the company's product line, brand image, brand positioning, or target market. Consumers evaluate CSR more positively if the fit is high (Becker-Olsen et al., 2006; Menon & Kahn, 2003; Speed & Thompson, 2000).

Holbrook (1978) elaborates that altruistic motives are much more likely to be perceived as authentic by customers if the CSR Fit of the CSR activity is high. Alhouti, Johnson and Holloway (2016) give an example for the reversed case when CSR Activities are perceived as hypocritical and, therefore, the fit influences inauthenticity. In the example, a company is selling a product that is harming the cause they simultaneously support regarding CSR. When a company engages in a CSR initiative because of motives that serve the public, it shows that it believes it is doing the right thing for society (Joo et al., 2019). A recent study proves that the perception of CSR fit is high when the company engages in social issues connected to its core business and advocates similar values or stakeholders (Austin & Gaither, 2019).

Furthermore, a high level of congruence speaks to the fact that a commitment to a social cause is not just for advertising purposes but is genuinely taken seriously by the company. Besides the fact that corporate motives are perceived as public good oriented (Kim & Lee, 2012), other positive influences of high fit are that consumers evaluate given information as more credible (Go & Bortree, 2017), increasing loyalty (Cha et al., 2016; Ham & Han, 2013) and purchase intentions (Elving, 2013). Therefore, the fit of a CSR initiative can play an essential role in consumer perceptions of authenticity (Fatma & Khan, 2022).

Following studies expanded the vital role of CSR fit in the determination of a CSR activity's effectiveness and related issues (Foreh & Grier, 2003; Sen & Bhattacharya, 2001). Researchers are curently showing that CSR fit is a crucial factor in the effectiveness of CSR (Harrison et al., 2022). Further studies observe that a higher CSR fit leads to a more positive evaluation by consumers

(Becker-Olsen et al., 2006; Harrison et al., 2022; Mazutis & Slawinski, 2015). Referring back to authenticity, it is crucial for a CSR activity to be congruent with a company's core values to be as authentic to key stakeholders as possible (Beckman et al., 2009; Mazutis & Slawinski, 2015). Alhouti, Johnson and Holloway (2016) add that fit is perceived as a characteristic of authenticity if the aforementioned logical alignment to the corporate concept and core business is given. A study by Alhouti, Johnson and Holloway (2016) shows the importance of CSR fit to the perception of CSR Authenticity. 17 % of Pérez's (2019) study participants report that inauthenticity is perceived when CSR fit is absent. Thus, there is a link between a company's CSR activities and its characteristics. The closer these two dimensions are to each other, the more positive the evaluation by consumers (Nan & Heo, 2007).

2.2.6. CSR Impact

The influence of CSR activities on social problems and their solutions is defined as CSR impact (Du et al., 2010). CSR impact is the importance of the social problem supported and the extent to which the CSR activity influences the solution for society or stakeholders (Alhouti et al., 2016). The impact can be measured by the number of people the CSR activity positively influences (Du et al., 2010; Joo et al., 2019) or the created benefit from supportive intentions for an organisation (Harrison et al., 2021) that stakeholders evaluate in relation to a firm's profits and size (Pérez, 2019). To research the concept of impact, often more measurable and practical variables are used, such as a donation amount (Grau & Folse, 2007; Zhu et al., 2017) or effort and commitment to the initiative (Du et al., 2010; Ellen et al., 2000).

Emphasizing the social impact of a company's CSR commitment or efforts is an effective communication strategy, as CSR communication should be realistic and avoid the impression of "bragging" (Sen et al., 2006). Positive influences of CSR Impact are the improvement of brand image, customer attitudes and satisfaction, attracting new customers and increasing purchase intentions (Maignan & Ferrell, 2004; Mulaessa & Wang, 2017) but more importantly for this study is the connection to the authenticity of CSR. According to Alhouti, Johnson and Holloway (2016), the Impact of CSR Activity negatively influences authenticity if the action is evaluated as ineffectual or excludes the important cause from a consumer perspective. That implies that a company's CSR activity is perceived as authentic in case a company can make a successful difference in society combined with a long-term commitment (Fatma & Khan, 2022). This statement shows the importance of CSR consistency and fit together as attributes of a CSR activity, which will be taken into account while constructing the conceptual model of this study.

Set in the context of persuasion knowledge theory (Friestad & Wright, 1994), it can be said that consumers evaluate CSR activities regarding the meaningfulness and the difference the activity makes with the help of the knowledge the consumer has about the social cause and the needed resources for a solution. Whether a consumer will perceive CSR engagement as authentic will rely on understanding the extent of the company's endeavours. This underlines the importance of further investigation of CSR impact in relation to Authenticity in practical examples like the fast fashion industry since current literature shows a real lack.

2.2.7. Brand Attitude

To explain the motivations and reasons of consumers that lead them to establish a relationship with a company and identify with it can be explained by theories such as social identity theory (Tajfel & Turner, 1979) or self-categorization theory (Turner et al., 1994). These theories state that consumer identification with a company is an influencing factor in relationship building. Further studies about customer-company identification include CSR activities in corporate identity as a significant part that can lead consumers to develop a feeling of relation with a company (Bhattacharya & Sen, 2003; Fatma & Rahman, 2016; Marin et al., 2009). CSR measures establish a connection between a consumer and a company. These measures are intended to portray the company's character and thus create a positive image and suggest to the consumer a sense of responsibility on the company's part (Marin et al., 2009). Companies are perceived more authentically when the social contribution comes from a company's own identity (van Rekom et al., 2014). Following these argumentations, consumers are assumed to be more likely to identify with a company if they perceive its CSR activities as authentic (Fatma & Khan, 2022).

Lastly, essential for developing a concept in this study are the findings of Kim and Lee (2019) in empirical research on how fit influences not only authenticity but also brand attitude. There, brand attitude is used for a consumer's attitude toward a brand and is the definition used for the following research framework. It is proven that CSR fit positively affects CSR authenticity and brand attitude, stating that authenticity mediates the relationship between CSR fit and brand attitude (Kim & Lee, 2019). Not only is this research reproducing the findings of Kim and Lee (2019) in a different industry, as suggested in their work, but it will also change the target group from only students to a broader population.

Additionally, two more attributes of a CSR activity are investigated in this concept to explore if the same meditation effect will occur.

2.3. Methodology

2.3.1. Hypotheses

The results of the literature review and previous research already showed relationships between different attributes of CSR activities, the authenticity of CSR, and the attitude toward a brand (Kim & Lee, 2019; Liu & Jung, 2021). Therefore, this paper develops a similar research framework to investigate the authenticity of CSR activities and the perceived brand image in the fast fashion industry. This study establishes the primary research framework based on the following hypotheses and investigates them.

Hypothesis 1 (H1): CSR attributes will have a positive effect on the authenticity of CSR.

Hypothesis 1-1 (H1-1). The consistency of CSR initiatives will positively affect the authenticity of CSR.

Hypothesis 1-2 (H1-2). The fit of CSR initiatives will positively affect the authenticity of CSR.

Hypothesis 1-3 (H1-3). The impact of CSR initiatives will positively affect the authenticity of CSR.

Hypothesis 2 (H2): CSR authenticity will have a mediating effect between the attributes of CSR and brand attitude.

Hypothesis 2-1 (H2-1): CSR authenticity will have a mediating effect between CSR consistency and brand attitude.

Hypothesis 2-2 (H2-2): CSR authenticity will have a mediating effect between CSR fit and brand attitude.

Hypothesis 2-3 (H2-3): CSR authenticity will have a mediating effect between CSR impact and brand attitude.

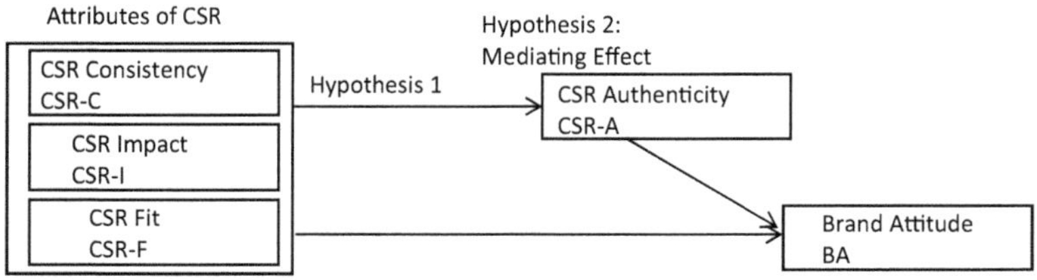

Figure 2.1: Conceptual model and hypotheses

2.3.2. Methods

The primary research of this study collected quantitative data on consumer perceptions with standardised interviews using the questionnaire survey method (Hameed et al., 2019) as a cross-sectional study, available online for one month.

In total 856 users took part in the online survey. A power analysis with the programme G-Power showed that the results would be significant from a number of 138 participants (Erdfelder et al., 2007), taking into account the work requirement and the mediative effect in the conceptual model (Fritz & Mackinnon, 2007). The desired power for this calculation was set very high at 0.95, whereas 0.8 would already be a high standard, and the value of 0.05 was given for the alpha error (Erdfelder et al., 2007). The effect size was set to standard 0.15, and the number of predictors is five, including two dependent and three independent variables.

For this study, three different cases of CSR activities of the leading fast fashion brands were created and tested. Each scenario contained items from previous literature. For the dependent variable brand attitude items were taken from Kim and Lee (2019). The items for independent variables CSR consistency were used from Liu and Jung (2021), CSR fit from Joo, Miller and Fink (2019) and CSR impact items were adopted from Joo, Miller and Fink (2019) and Liu and Jung (2021). Studies have successfully reused CSR authenticity items from Alhouti, Johnson and Holloway (2016) which were used for the mediating variable in this study. As scale rating a five-point Likert scale rating was used following a quantitative study framework to measure these items. As control variables, individual interaction with each brand (Joo et al., 2019) and demographic data, including age, gender, ethnicity, and current residence, were asked.

2.4. Data Presentation, Analysis and Discussion

2.4.1. Sample, Reliability and Correlation

The data collected for this study was cleaned according to selected criteria (age, duplicates, consistency, and duration) to obtain a database that is as representative as possible. This led to an adjustment of 585 representative responses. The average respondent is female, 30 years old, White / Caucasian, and from the United States of America or Europe which correlates with the typical fast fashion target group.

All values for Cronbach's Alpha in every Case are above the threshold of 0.7 as to be seen in Tables 2.1, 2.2 and 2.3, indicating a reliable construct (Nunnally, 1967; Saunders et al., 2014).

Table 2.1: Correlation and reliability analysis (Case 1: H&M)

Attributes	CSR-C	CSR-F	CSR-I	CSR-A	BA	Cronbach's α
CSR-C	1					0.724
CSR-F	0.765**	1				0.818
CSR-I	0.787**	0.782**	1			0.805
CSR-A	0.816**	0.828**	0.817**	1		0.837
BA	0.706**	0.640**	0.661**	0.676**	1	0.794

N=585; **p <0.01 (2-tailed test)

Table 2.2: Correlation and reliability analysis (Case 2: Zara)

Attributes	CSR-C	CSR-F	CSR-I	CSR-A	BA	Cronbach's α
CSR-C	1					0.738
CSR-F	0.736**	1				0.820
CSR-I	0.823**	0.804**	1			0.820
CSR-A	0.782**	0.844**	0.812**	1		0.837
BA	0.658**	0.644**	0.709**	0.670**	1	0.841

N=585; **p <0.01 (2-tailed test)

Table 2.3: Correlation and reliability analysis (Case 3: Uniqlo)

Attributes	CSR-C	CSR-F	CSR-I	CSR-A	BA	Cronbach's α
CSR-C	1					0.731
CSR-F	0.693**	1				0.811
CSR-I	0.763**	0.792**	1			0.784
CSR-A	0.728**	0.816**	0.773**	1		0.817
BA	0.637**	0.551**	0.621**	0.583**	1	0.854

N=585; **p <0.01 (2-tailed test)

Table 2.4 offers a description of the variables and items in connection with the three case studies. A confirmatory factor analysis was performed using IBM SPSS AMOS 26, and the standardised factor loading of all items shown in Table 2.1 were significant and above the threshold of 0.5, which confirms

Table 2.4: Variables and item description

Variables	Items	Case 1: H&M Group		Case 2: Zara		Case 3: Uniqlo	
		Mean (Standard Deviation)	Factor loadings	Mean (Standard Deviation)	Factor loadings	Mean (Standard Deviation)	Factor loadings
CSR-C	The brand has been actively practising CSR for a long time.	3.9772 (0.68208)	0.667	3.9538 (0.67571)	0.696	3.8621 (0.68495)	0.690
	The brand continuously engages in CSR.		0.664		0.664		0.648
	The brand is consistently performing CSR activities.		0.721		0.735		0.732
CSR-F	The brand and the described CSR activity fit together well.	3.8167 (0.73358)	0.722	3.7812 (0.72857)	0.717	3.6457 (0.77982)	0.680
	There is a logical connection between the brand and the described CSR activity.		0.744		0.731		0.739
	The described CSR activity seems to align well with the brand.		0.709		0.733		0.737
	The described CSR activity and the brand seem compatible.		0.737		0.740		0.728

(*Continued*)

Table 2.4: Continued

Variables	Items	Case 1: H&M Group		Case 2: Zara		Case 3: Uniqlo	
		Mean (Standard Deviation)	**Factor loadings**	**Mean (Standard Deviation)**	**Factor loadings**	**Mean (Standard Deviation)**	**Factor loadings**
CSR-I	The brand's contribution to solving the social problem is significant.	3.8312 (0.70090)	0.754	3.8021 (0.73854)	0.731	3.7282 (0.70107)	0.708
	The brand's contribution to solving the social problem is high.		0.713		0.718		0.669
	The Impact of the CSR activity is sufficient to be noteworthy.		0.671		0.732		0.670
	The brand's CSR activities contribute to solving the social problem in the long term.		0.714		0.738		0.714
CSR A	The company's CSR actions are genuine.	3.8167 (0.74602)	0.750	3.7825 (0.74385)	0.739	3.6718 (0.74855)	0.732
	The company's CSR action is in accordance with the company's values and beliefs.		0.754		0.722		0.703
	The company is a socially responsible company.		0.745		0.769		0.731
	The company is concerned about improving the well-being of society.		0.748		0.774		0.738
BA	I like the products of this brand.	4.0462 (0.73582)	0.770	3.9687 (0.80427)	0.809	3.9379 (0.81401)	0.837
	I like the service of this brand.		0.764		0.791		0.804
	I trust the quality of this brand's products.		0.721		0.797		0.799

a convergent validity (Liu & Jung, 2021). A Reliability analysis examines the internal consistency of a model using Cronbach's alpha coefficient to determine the measurements' reliability (Koufteros, 1999).

The statistical analysis findings on the variables' correlation show that the attributes of CSR activities correlate moderately to strongly with CSR authenticity and brand attitude for the three presented cases. In the literature research of this work, it was observed that previous studies also describe the correlation of CSR attributes with CSR authenticity and brand attitude (Fatma & Khan, 2022; Joo et al., 2019; Latif et al., 2022; Liu & Jung, 2021). It is noticeable that CSR fit correlates very strongly with CSR authenticity in all three cases, as indicated by previous research (Fatma & Khan, 2022; Harrison et al., 2022; Pérez, 2019). This means that the Fit of CSR activities and authenticity are strongly related from the consumers' point of view.

2.4.2. Hypothesis H1: Multiple Regression Analysis

The regression analysis results show that in all three cases, the dependent variable is statistically significantly positively affected by the independent variables. It results that in the first Case CSR-I (β=0.373, t=11.0096) has a larger effect than CSR-C (β=0.339, t=9.280) and CSR-F (β=0.304, t=8.270). In the second case, the effect of CSR-I (β=0.501, t=14.629) is even stronger compared to CSR-C (β=0.264, t=6.822) and CSR-F (β=0.222, t=5.501). Also, in the third case, the regression coefficient of CSR-C (β=0.474, t=13.610) is higher than the variables CSR-C (β=0.247, t=6.579) and CSR-I (β=0.223, t=5.159). These results confirm the first hypothesis, H1, including all three sub-hypotheses, H1-1, H1-2 and H1-3, of this study, which state that the Attributes CSR-C, CSR-F, and CSR-I have a positive effect on CSR-A, is supported. The higher the consistency, fit and impact of a CSR activity, the greater the CSR authenticity consumers perceive.

The three sub-hypotheses H1-1, H1-2 and H1-3 on the respective attributes of CSR activities and their positive influence on authenticity could all be confirmed using multiple regression analysis. This means that the primary hypothesis H1 is fully supported, and CSR activities positively affect CSR authenticity in consumers' perception. Regarding hypotheses H1-1 and H1-2, the study of Liu and Jung (2021) partially comes to a different conclusion. The significance of CSR sustainability (Consistency) and CSR fit is only seen in the simple regression analysis. In contrast, CSR consistency and CSR fit are consistently significant in all three cases in this study. In the literature, the consideration of consistency of CSR activities is recognised as very relevant in relation to the research of CSR authenticity and consumer perception (Beckman et al., 2009; Yoo & Lee, 2018).

By demonstrating the significance of CSR consistency, this study was able to make a further contribution to the attribute that has been under-researched so far. Hypothesis H1-3 on CSR impact is significant in the findings of Liu and Jung (2021) and this study.

Table 2.5: Multiple regression analysis (Case 1: H&M)

Dependent Variable	Independent Variable	$R^2$5	Adjusted R2	F	β	*t*-Test
CSR-A	CSR-C	0.790	0.789	729.145	0.339	9.280***
	CSR-F				0.304	8.270***
	CSR-I				0.373	11.096***

**p <0.01; ***p<0.001

Table 2.6: Multiple regression analysis (Case 2: Zara)

Dependent Variable	Independent Variable	R^2	Adjusted R2	F	β	*t*-Test
CSR-A	CSR-C	0.780	0.779	685.997	0.264	6.822***
	CSR-F				0.220	5.501***
	CSR-I				0.501	14.629***

**p <0.01; ***p<0.001

Table 2.7: Multiple regression analysis (Case 3: Uniqlo)

Dependent Variable	Independent Variable	R^2	Adjusted R2	F	β	*t*-Test
CSR-A	CSR-C	0.729	0.728	521.337	0.247	6.579***
	CSR-F				0.223	5.159***
	CSR-I				0.474	13.610***

**p <0.01; ***p<0.001

2.4.3. Hypothesis H2: Mediation Regression Analysis

Mediation analysis is performed in Hayes' Model 4 to test the mediating relationship described in hypothesis H2. The analysis was performed for each sub-hypotheses H2-1, H2-2 and H2-3 in every case. The confidence interval was left at the default level of 95 %, as was the number of 5000 samples for bootstrapping.

According to Baron and Kenny (1986), the four paths *c* (combined direct and indirect effect), *a* (X→M), *b* (M→Y), and *c'* (direct effect) have to be significant to prove a mediating effect. The results for the paths *a*, *b*, *c'* (direct) and *ab* as standardised indirect effects are shown in the result Tables 2.8 to 2.16 for every independent variable in each case.

First, it is essential to state that all mediation analysis results are significant, as the p values are under the threshold of 0.05. Furthermore, the confidence levels from the bootstrapping do not contain zero, implying that the indirect paths all describe a mediation effect. These findings show that CSR authenticity fully mediates the relationship between CSR attributes and brand attitude in every case, and hypothesis H2 is fully supported. This means that authenticity has a mediating effect on the relationship between CSR consistency, CSR fit, and CSR impact of CSR activities and consumers' brand attitude. In the study by Kim and Lee (2019), partial mediation between CSR fit and brand attitude by CSR authenticity has already been shown. This study extends the concept of CSR attributes to include the relevance of CSR consistency and impact. In line with Fatma and Khan (2022), who argued that consumers are more likely to identify with a company whose CSR activities are perceived as authentic, this study was able to show that authenticity does have a mediating role in the relationship between attributes of CSR activities and brand attitude. When considering consumer identification and the influence of CSR activities on it (Fatma & Rahman, 2016; Marin et al., 2009), the mediator role of CSR authenticity should be considered. Expanding on the theories of social identity (Tajfel & Turner, 1979) and self-categorizing (Turner et al., 1994), it can be stated that CSR authenticity has an influence on the relationship building between customers and companies.

Table 2.8: Mediation analysis CSR-C (Case 1: H&M)

	Paths in Mediation	β	*t*	*P*	R	R^2
CSR-C/	CSR-C → CSR-A	0.8921	34.0429	0.0000*	0.8157	0.6653
CSR-A/	CSR-A → BA	0.2973	6.1257	0.0000*	0.7269	0.5284
BA	CSR-C → BA	0.4961	9.3451	0.0000*	0.7057	0.4980
	CSR-C*CSR-A → BA	0.2459	CI[a] = [0.1598, 0.3401]			

[a] CI = 95 % confidence level (bootstrapping), *p<0.05

Table 2.9: Mediation analysis CSR-F (Case 1: H&M)

	Paths in Mediation	B	*t*	*P*	R	R^2
CSR-F/ CSR-A/ BA	CSR-F →CSR-A	0.8417	35.6082	0.0000*	0.8277	0.6850
	CSR-A →BA	0.4587	8.7160	0.0000*	0.6915	0.4782
	CSR-F →BA	0.2563	4.7886	0.0000*	0.6404	0.4101
	CSR-F*CSR-A →BA	0.3849	CI[a] = [0.2874, 0.4896]			

[A] CI = 95 % confidence level (bootstrapping), *p<0.05

Table 2.10: Mediation analysis CSR-I (Case 1: H&M)

	Paths in Mediation	B	*t*	*p*	R	R^2
CSR-I/ CSR-A/ BA	CSR-I →CSR-A	0.8693	34.1742	0.0000*	0.8167	0.6670
	CSR-A →BA	0.4036	8.0026	0.0000*	0.7023	0.4933
	CSR-I →BA	0.3436	6.3998	0.0000*	0.6615	0.4375
	CSR-I*CSR-A →BA	0.3342	CI[a] = [0.2497, 0.4207]			

[A] CI = 95 % confidence level (bootstrapping), *p<0.05

Table 2.11: Mediation analysis CSR-C (Case 2: Zara)

	Paths in Mediation	β	*t*	*p*	R	R^2
CSR-C/ CSR-A/ BA	CSR-C →CSR-A	0.8606	30.2664	0.0000*	0.7817	0.6111
	CSR-A →BA	0.4335	8.4917	0.0000*	0.7039	0.4954
	CSR-C →BA	0.4101	7.2975	0.0000*	0.6580	0.4329
	CSR-C*CSR-A →BA	0.3134	CI[a] = [0.2347, 0.3905]			

[A] CI = 95 % confidence level (bootstrapping), *p<0.05

Table 2.12: Mediation analysis CSR-F (Case 2: Zara)

	Paths in Mediation	β	*T*	*p*	R	R^2
CSR-F/ CSR-A/ BA	CSR-F →CSR-A	0.8614	37.9515	0.0000*	0.8437	0.7119
	CSR-A →BA	0.4752	7.8242	0.0000*	0.6862	0.4708
	CSR-F →BA	0.3019	4.8685	0.0000*	0.6443	0.4152
	CSR-F*CSR-A →BA	0.3708	CI[a] = [0.2658, 0.4743]			

[A] CI = 95 % confidence level (bootstrapping), *p<0.05

Table 2.13: Mediation analysis CSR-I (Case 2: Zara)

	Paths in Mediation	β	*T*	*p*	R	R^2
CSR-I/	CSR-I →CSR-A	0.8174	33.5441	0.0000*	0.8116	0.6587
CSR-A/	CSR-A →BA	0.3004	5.7051	0.0000*	0.7274	0.5291
BA	CSR-I →BA	0.5266	9.9317	0.0000*	0.7090	0.5027
	CSR-I*CSR-A →BA	0.2255	CI[a] = [0.1307, 0.3198]			

[A] CI = 95 % confidence level (bootstrapping), *$p<0.05$

Table 2.14: Mediation analysis CSR- C (Case 3: Uniqlo)

	Paths in Mediation	B	*t*	*p*	R	R^2
CSR-C/	CSR-C →CSR-A	0.7951	25.6078	0.0000*	0.7276	0.5294
CSR-A/	CSR-A →BA	0.2769	5.6107	0.0000*	0.6602	0.4359
BA	CSR-C →BA	0.5365	9.9485	0.0000*	0.6367	0.4054
	CSR-C*CSR-A →BA	0.1853	CI[a] = [0.1045, 0.2670]			

[A] CI = 95 % confidence level (bootstrapping), *$p<0.05$

Table 2.15: Mediation analysis CSR- F (Case 3: Uniqlo)

	Paths in Mediation	B	*T*	*p*	R	R^2
CSR-F/	CSR-F →CSR-A	0.7834	34.1043	0.0000*	0.8162	0.6661
CSR-A/	CSR-A →BA	0.4342	6.9408	0.0000*	0.5974	0.3569
BA	CSR-F →BA	0.2351	3.9149	0.0001*	0.5511	0.3037
	CSR-F*CSR-A →BA	0.3259	CI[a] = [0.2282, 0.4259]			

[A] CI = 95 % confidence level (bootstrapping), *$p<0.05$

Table 2.16: Mediation analysis CSR- I (Case 3: Uniqlo)

	Paths in Mediation	B	*T*	*p*	R	R^2
CSR-I/	CSR-I →CSR-A	0.8253	29.4116	0.0000*	0.7729	0.5974
CSR-A/	CSR-A →BA	0.2775	5.0961	0.0000*	0.6422	0.4125
BA	CSR-I →BA	0.4926	8.4724	0.0000*	0.6215	0.3862
	CSR-I*CSR-A →BA	0.1972	CI[a] = [0.1121, 0.2882]			

[A] CI = 95 % confidence level (bootstrapping), *$p<0.05$

2.5. Conclusion and Recommendations

2.5.1. Knowledge Contributions

For companies, CSR activities have become essential for corporate competitiveness (Porter & Kramer, 2007, 2011). Managers are faced with the challenge of integrating the phenomenon of CSR into corporate strategy (Choi et al., 2019; Rodriguez-Gomez et al., 2020). Based on this strategy, concepts for its implementation are developed, measures adopted, and resources allocated. From the perspective of the consumer and other stakeholders, the authenticity of the design of the CSR engagement is of central importance (Afzali & Kim, 2021; Fatma & Khan, 2022; Liu & Jung, 2021). Ideally, decision-makers rely on a scientifically based general theory or practically tested concepts. This study makes a scientific contribution to the generation of empirical evidence and the development of an understanding of the underlying mechanisms of authenticity in the context of CSR. A positive effect of attributes of CSR activities on consumer perceptions of CSR authenticity and the mediative role of authenticity on brand attitude in the context of fast fashion was established.

The result of the literature review and the consideration of the empirical studies indicate that the research field has grown and matured significantly in recent years (Ji et al., 2022) without a general theorization on authenticity being available. As a result, the CSR attributes of consistency, fit, and impact could be identified as influencing factors of perceived CSR authenticity from the available findings of mainly empirical research. In addition, consumers' relationship with the company and perceptions of CSR authenticity was shown to be in relation to brand attitude (Fatma & Khan, 2022; Marin et al., 2009).

The empirical investigation, in the form of an online survey, using the self-developed conceptual model and questionnaire, confirmed the two hypotheses and sub-hypotheses established in the context of the fast fashion industry. Hypothesis H1 approved the positive effect of the attributes of CSR activities on CSR authenticity. Another result is the confirmation of hypothesis H2, which describes the mediative role of authenticity in the relationship between CSR attributes and brand attitude.

The findings of this study enrich the current state of research on authenticity and CSR. First, they support previous statements in the literature regarding the relevance and relationships of CSR attributes, authenticity, and brand attitude (Alhouti et al., 2016; Joo et al., 2019; Kim & Lee, 2019; Liu & Jung, 2021). Second, the conceptual model on authenticity has further developed and focused on previous hypothesis models so that it can now be used for further empirical research. Third, previous research findings of CSR authenticity have been replicated for the fast fashion industry, thus providing the basis for further in-depth research in the specific industry. Fourth, the successful replication for the fast fashion industry is also recommended for further empirical research to apply to other industries and companies. Fifth, by including additional scientific disciplines from the theoretical framework of authenticity, a step has been made toward an interdependent view of the phenomenon of CSR authenticity. Overall, the key findings of this study provide, on the one hand, a further basis for the progressive development of a general theory of authenticity. On the other hand, empirical research can use the results for further studies.

A general theory of authenticity claims to make universal statements about the real-world phenomenon of authenticity (Popper, 1959). Therefore, specific statements that are only correct in a particular situation are not suitable as a general theory. Models often represent the theoretical consideration of individual sections of reality (Mayntz, 1967). Explanatory models, which are continually adapted, help to differentiate a theory further and make it more accurate (Dörner, 1984). Resulting from this, the conceptual model used in this study is an explanatory model that has been adapted and further developed from the literature. Subsequently, this model should be further replicated and, if necessary, refined in the direction of universal statements. Due to the complexity and multidimensionality of the phenomenon of authenticity, an interdisciplinary approach is needed. The first approaches to combining economic research results with other scientific disciplines are the social psychological attribution theory (Heider, 1946) and psychological Bayesian models of cognition (Perfors et al., 2011).

2.5.2. Industry Recommendations

It can be said that the findings of this study fundamentally support the industry in integrating the phenomenon of CSR into corporate strategy. It is an advantage that the formulated empirical findings are based on consumers' perceptions. Furthermore, the individual results are also based on the concrete survey of specific cases/companies, which is conducive to practical relevance and acceptance. First, this applies to companies with a similar profile as in the cases. A limitation is given by the fact that the findings are individual aspects and not a general theory. Furthermore, due to the importance and complexity of the phenomenon (Song & Dong, 2022), the perception and interests of other stakeholders must be taken into account in addition to consumers (Du et al., 2015; Kim & Lee, 2019).

Specific recommendations can be derived based on the results from applying the conceptual model on authenticity and the confirmed hypotheses. Consumers' perceptions of the positive effect of attributes of CSR activities on CSR authenticity should be considered in the strategy and the CSR activities derived from it. Due to the consistently high significance of the CSR fit attribute, it is essential to ensure that CSR activities take this into account when recommending actions. Furthermore, it is important that the CSR activities are consistent and that consumers perceive noticeable impacts from the CSR activities. From the confirmed hypothesis H2, it follows that a mediative role of authenticity in the relationship of CSR attributes to brand attitude is given. Accordingly, it is important to pay attention to not only the attributes of CSR activities but also the perception of authenticity for the brand attitude or image of the company. This is all the more so because authenticity in CSR describes the potential of how CSR can create value for the company, stakeholders, and society (Song & Dong, 2022).

In the literature, the perception of authenticity is increasingly seen as the perception of truth (Grayson & Martinec, 2004; Morhart et al., 2015). In the study, therefore, the two types of ideal truth and self-truth were assumed for the respondents' perceptions. The exclusion of the true-to-fact type, which also occurs, offers companies the potential to consider this in their framework for action. Accordingly, CSR activities are considered true or more authentic when transparent and accessible facts are available. From the response to the survey, a characteristic target group has emerged that is receptive to the use of social media. For companies, this means a significant opportunity to communicate facts about CSR activities to characteristic target group of consumers.

2.6. Limitations and Further Research

In this study, data was collected using the JISC online survey tool, which has technical limitations that may affect the results. It is therefore recommended to replicate the framework of this study using a tool that allows for randomization of questions/cases and does not allow for repeated participation. Replications of previous studies can further strengthen the results, especially recommended for other industries and more different developed cases.

This study's methodological approach allowed the investigation of a relationship between the CSR attributes, authenticity, and brand attitude. Further research should also utilize other methodological choices and strategies, such as qualitative consumer interviews, to understand the "why" of the relationships in addition to the investigated "what" and "how". Also, how the different CSR attributes influence each other and how big the influences on authenticity should be further investigated.

The mediation analysis of authenticity between CSR attributes and brand attitude was significant however, the exact effect can be described more deeply in future studies. Also, what exactly mediation means for consumer behaviour in terms of identification with and relationship to the brand is further interesting to understand.

For this study, three different Cases on the CSR activities of the leading fast fashion brands were created and tested. Companies with high brand awareness and large financial resources tend to be economically possible to invest more in CSR activities. However, whether this positively affects the authenticity of the CSR commitment or whether small and medium-sized companies are perceived more authentically would require further research. Furthermore, the criterion of market share and industry was chosen in this study. In future studies, other or combinations of the selection criteria of the brands can be investigated, for example, region or product.

In general, it can be said that the research gap and the lack of theoretical models on Authenticity result in a general recommendation for further research in this area.

References

Afzali, H. & Kim, S. S. (2021). Consumers' Responses to Corporate Social Responsibility: The Mediating Role of CSR Authenticity. *Sustainability*, 13 (4), p. 2224.

Alhouti, S. & D'Souza, G. (2018). Benefits of Corporate Social Responsibility. *Journal of Consumer Marketing*, 35 (3), pp. 277–286.

Alhouti, S., Johnson, C. M. & Holloway, B. B. (2016). Corporate Social Responsibility Authenticity: Investigating Its Antecedents and Outcomes. *Journal of Business Research*, 69 (3), pp. 1242–1249.

Austin, L. & Gaither, B. M. (2019). Redefining Fit: Examining CSR Company-Issue Fit in Stigmatized Industries. *Journal of Brand Management*, 26 (1), pp. 9–20.

Baron, R. M. & Kenny, D. A. (1986). The Moderator-Mediator Variable Distinction in Social Psychological Research: Conceptual, Strategic, and Statistical Considerations. *Journal of Personality And Social Psychology*, 51 (6), pp. 1173–1182.

Becker-Olsen, K. L., Cudmore, B. A. & Hill, R. P. (2006). The Impact of Perceived Corporate Social Responsibility on Consumer Behavior. *Journal of Business Research*, 59 (1), pp. 46–53.

Beckman, T., Colwell, A. & Cunningham, P. H. (2009). The Emergence of Corporate Social Responsibility in Chile: The Importance of Authenticity and Social Networks. *Journal of Business Ethics*, 86 (S2), pp. 191–206.

Bhardwaj, B. R. (2016). Role of Green Policy on Sustainable Supply Chain Management. *Benchmarking: An International Journal*, 23 (2), pp. 456–468.

Bhardwaj, V. & Fairhurst, A. (2010). Fast Fashion: Response to Changes in the Fashion Industry. *The International Review of Retail, Distribution and Consumer Research*, 20 (1), pp. 165–173.

Bhattacharya, C. B. & Sen, S. (2003). Consumer – Company Identification: A Framework for Understanding Consumers' Relationships with Companies. *Journal of Marketing*, 67 (2), pp. 76–88.

Brashier, N. M. & Marsh, E. J. (2020). Judging Truth. *Annual Review of Psychology*, 71 (1), pp. 499–515.

Brown, S., Kozinets, R. V. & Sherry, J. F. (2003). Teaching Old Brands New Tricks: Retro Branding and the Revival of Brand Meaning. *Journal of Marketing*, 67 (3), pp. 19–33.

Carroll, A. B. (1979). A Three-Dimensional Conceptual Model of Corporate Performance. *The Academy of Management Review*, 4 (4), pp. 497.

Carroll, A. B. (2016). Carroll's Pyramid of CSR: Taking Another Look. *International Journal of Corporate Social Responsibility*, 1 (1).

Cha, M.-K., Yi, Y. & Bagozzi, R. P. (2016). Effects of Customer Participation in Corporate Social Responsibility (CSR) Programs on the CSR-Brand Fit and Brand Loyalty. *Cornell Hospitality Quarterly*, 57 (3), pp. 235–249.

Chiu, H.-C., Hsieh, Y.-C. & Kuo, Y.-C. (2012). How to Align Your Brand Stories with Your Products. *Journal of Retailing*, 88 (2), pp. 262–275.

Choi, D., Chung, C. Y. & Young, J. (2019). An Economic Analysis of Corporate Social Responsibility in Korea. *Sustainability*, 11 (9), pp. 2676.

Cohen, J. (1992). Quantitative Methods in Psychology: A Power Primer. *Psychological Bulletin*. Citeseer.

Dörner, D. (1984). Denken, Problemlösen und Intelligenz. *Psychologische Rundschau*, 35 (1), pp. 1020.

Driver, M. (2006). Beyond the Stalemate of Economics versus Ethics: Corporate Social Responsibility and the Discourse of the Organizational Self. *Journal of Business Ethics*, 66 (4), pp. 337–356.

Drumwright, M. E. (1996). Company Advertising with a Social Dimension: The Role of Noneconomic Criteria. *Journal of Marketing*, 60 (4), pp. 71.

Du, S., Bhattacharya, C. B. & Sen, S. (2007). Reaping Relational Rewards from Corporate Social Responsibility: The Role of Competitive Positioning. *International Journal of Research in Marketing*, 24 (3), pp. 224–241.

Du, S., Bhattacharya, C. B. & Sen, S. (2010). Maximizing Business Returns to Corporate Social Responsibility (CSR): The Role of CSR Communication. *International Journal of Management Reviews*, 12 (1), pp. 8–19.

Du, S., Bhattacharya, C. B. & Sen, S. (2015). Corporate Social Responsibility, Multi-faceted Job-Products, and Employee Outcomes. *Journal of Business Ethics*, 131 (2), pp. 319–335.

Edelman. (2022). *Edelman Trust Barometer 2022*. https://www.edelman.com/trust/2022-trust-barometer

Ellen, P. S., Mohr, L. A. & Webb, D. J. (2000). Charitable Programs and the Retailer: Do They Mix?. *Journal of Retailing*, 76 (3), pp. 393–406.

Ellen, P. S., Webb, D. J. & Mohr, L. A. (2006). Building Corporate Associations: Consumer Attributions for Corporate Socially Responsible Programs. *Journal of the Academy of Marketing Science*, 34 (2), pp. 147–157.

Elving, W. J. L. (2013). Scepticism and Corporate Social Responsibility Communications: The Influence of Fit and Reputation. *Journal of Marketing Communications*, 19 (4), pp. 277–292.

Erdfelder, E., Faul, F. & Buchner, A. (2007). G*Power 3: A Flexible Statistical Power Analysis Program for the Social, Behavioral, and Biomedical Sciences. *Behavior Research Methods*, 39 (2), pp. 175–191.

European Commission. (2001). *Green Paper*. Commission of European Union. https://eur-lex.europa.eu/LexUriServ/LexUriServ.do?uri=COM:2001:0366:FIN:EN:PDF%20.

Fatma, M. & Khan, I. (2022). An Investigation of Consumer Evaluation of Authenticity of Their Company's CSR Engagement. *Total Quality Management & Business Excellence*, 33 (1–2), pp. 55–72.

Fatma, M. & Rahman, Z. (2016). The CSR's Influence on Customer Responses in Indian Banking Sector. *Journal of Retailing and Consumer Services*, 29, pp. 49–57.

Foreh, M. R. & Grier, S. (2003). When Is Honesty the Best Policy? The Effect of Stated Company Intent on Consumer Scepticism. *Journal of Consumer Psychology*, 13 (3), pp. 349–356.

Friestad, M. & Wright, P. (1994). The Persuasion Knowledge Model: How People Cope with Persuasion Attempts. *Journal of Consumer Research*, 21 (1), pp. 1.

Fritz, M. S. & Mackinnon, D. P. (2007). Required Sample Size to Detect the Mediated Effect. *Psychological Science*, 18 (3), pp. 233–239.

Go, E. & Bortree, D. S. (2017). What and How to Communicate CSR? The Role of CSR fit, Modality Interactivity, and Message Interactivity on Social Networking Sites. *Journal of Promotion Management*, 23 (5), pp. 727–747.

Grau, S. L. & Folse, J. A. G. (2007). Cause-Related Marketing (CRM): The Influence of Donation Proximity and Message-Framing Cues on the Less-Involved Consumer. *Journal of Advertising*, 36 (4), pp. 19–33.

Grayson, K. & Martinec, R. (2004). Consumer Perceptions of Iconicity and Indexicality and Their Influence on Assessments of Authentic Market Offerings. *Journal of Consumer Research*, 31 (2), pp. 296–312.

Groza, M. D., Pronschinske, M. R. & Walker, M. (2011). Perceived Organizational Motives and Consumer Responses to Proactive and Reactive CSR. *Journal of Business Ethics*, 102 (4), pp. 639–652.

Gupta, S. & Pirsch, J. (2006). The Company-Cause-Customer Fit Decision in Cause-Related Marketing. *Journal of Consumer Marketing*, 23 (6), pp. 314–326.

H&M-Group. (2022b). *Supply Chain*. https://hmgroup.com/sustainability/leading-the-change/transparency/supply-chain/

H&M-Group. (2022c). *Store Count Per Brand*. https://hmgroup.com/about-us/markets-and-expansion/store-count-per-brand/

H&M-Group. (2022d). *H&M Group – History*. https://hmgroup.com/about-us/history/

H&M-Group (2022e). *Cotton*. https://hmgroup.com/sustainability/circular-and-climate-positive/materials/cotton/

Ham, S. & Han, H. (2013). Role of Perceived Fit With Hotels' Green Practices in the Formation of Customer Loyalty: Impact of Environmental Concerns. *Asia Pacific Journal of Tourism Research*, 18 (7), pp. 731–748.

Hameed, Z., Khan, I. U., Islam, T., Sheikh, Z. & Khan, S. U. (2019). Corporate Social Responsibility and Employee Pro-Environmental Behaviors. *South Asian Journal of Business Studies*, 8 (3), pp. 246–265.

Harrison, V., Vafeiadis, M., Diddi, P. & Conlin, J. (2021). The Impact of CSR on Nonprofit Outcomes: How the Choice of Corporate Partner Influences Reputation and Supportive Intentions. *Corporate Communications: An International Journal*, 27 (2), pp. 205–225.

Harrison, V. S., Vafeiadis, M. & Bober, J. (2022). Greening Professional Sport: How Communicating the Fit, Proximity, and Impact of Sustainability Efforts Affects Fan Perceptions and Supportive Intentions. *Sustainability*, 14 (6), p. 3139.

Hayes, A. F. (2009). Beyond Baron and Kenny: Statistical Mediation Analysis in the New Millennium. *Communication Monographs*, 76 (4), pp. 408–420.

Heider, F. (1946). Attitudes and Cognitive Organization. *The Journal of Psychology*, 21 (1), pp. 107–112.

Holbrook, M. B. (1978). Beyond Attitude Structure: Toward the Informational Determinants of Attitude. *Journal of Marketing Research*, 15 (4), p. 545.

Jalilvand, M. R., Nasrolahi Vosta, L., Kazemi Mahyari, H. & Khazaei Pool, J. (2017). Social Responsibility Influence on Customer Trust in Hotels: Mediating Effects of Reputation and Word-of-Mouth. *Tourism Review*, 72 (1), pp. 1–14.

Jarvis, W., Ouschan, R., Burton, H. J., Soutar, G. & O'Brien, I. M. (2017). Customer Engagement in CSR: A Utility Theory Model with Moderating Variables. *Journal of Service Theory and Practice*, 27 (4), pp. 833–853.

Ji, Y. G., Tao, W. & Rim, H. (2022). Theoretical Insights of CSR Research in Communication from 1980 to 2018: A Bibliometric Network Analysis. *Journal of Business Ethics*, 177 (2), pp. 327–349.

Joo, S., Miller, E. G. & Fink, J. S. (2019). Consumer Evaluations of CSR Authenticity: Development and Validation of a Multidimensional CSR Authenticity Scale. *Journal of Business Research*, 98, pp. 236–249.

Jose, S., Khare, N. & Buchanan, F. R. (2018). Customer Perceptions of CSR Authenticity. *International Journal of Organizational Analysis*, 26 (4), pp. 614–629.

Kelley, H. H. (1973). The Processes of Causal Attribution. *American Psychologist*, 28 (2), p. 107.

Kernis, M. H. & Goldman, B. M. (2006). A Multicomponent Conceptualization of Authenticity: Theory and Research. In *Advances in Experimental Social Psychology* (pp. 283–357). Academic Press.

Khan, M., Serafeim, G. & Yoon, A. (2016). Corporate Sustainability: First Evidence on Materiality. *The Accounting Review*, 91 (6), pp. 1697–1724.

Kim, C., Kim, J., Marshall, R. & Afzali, H. (2018). Stakeholder Influence, Institutional Duality, and CSR Involvement of MNC Subsidiaries. *Journal of Business Research*, 91 pp. 40–47.

Kim, S. & Lee, H. (2019). The Effect of CSR Fit and CSR Authenticity on the Brand Attitude. *Sustainability*, 12 (1), p. 275.

Kim, S. & Lee, Y.-J. (2012). The Complex Attribution Process of CSR Motives. *Public Relations Review*, 38 (1), pp. 168–170.

Kirchoff, J. F., Tate, W. L. & Mollenkopf, D. A. (2016). The Impact of Strategic Organizational Orientations on Green Supply Chain Management and Firm Performance. *International Journal of Physical Distribution & Logistics Management*, 46 (3), pp. 269–292.

Koufteros, X. A. (1999). Testing a Model of Pull Production: A Paradigm for Manufacturing Research Using Structural Equation Modeling. *Journal of Operations Management*, 17 (4), pp. 467–488.

Kovács, B. (2019). Authenticity Is in the Eye of the Beholder: The Exploration of Audiences' Lay Associations to Authenticity Across Five Domains. *Review of General Psychology*, 23 (1), pp. 32–59.

L'Etang, J. (1994). Public Relations and Corporate Social Responsibility: Some Issues Arising. *Journal of Business Ethics*, 13 (2), pp. 111–123.

Latif, B., Ong, T. S., Meero, A., Abdul Rahman, A. A. & Ali, M. (2022). Employee-Perceived Corporate Social Responsibility (CSR) and Employee Pro-Environmental Behavior (PEB): The Moderating Role of CSR Skepticism and CSR Authenticity. *Sustainability*, 14 (3), pp. 1380.

Laufer, W. S. (2003). Social Accountability and Corporate Greenwashing. *Journal of Business Ethics*, 43 (3), pp. 253–261.

Lii, Y.-S. & Lee, M. (2012). Doing Right Leads to Doing Well: When the Type of CSR and Reputation Interact to Affect Consumer Evaluations of the Firm. *Journal of Business Ethics*, 105 (1), pp. 69–81.

Liu, H. & Jung, J.-S. (2021). The Effect of CSR Attributes on CSR Authenticity: Focusing on Mediating Effects of Digital Transformation. *Sustainability*, 13 (13), p. 7206.

Lo, A. (2020). Effects of Customer Experience in Engaging in Hotels' CSR Activities on Brand Relationship Quality and Behavioural Intention. *Journal of Travel & Tourism Marketing*, 37 (2), pp. 185–199.

Losada-Otálora, M. & Alkire (née Nasr), L. (2019). Investigating the Transformative Impact of Bank Transparency on Consumers' Financial Well-Being. *International Journal of Bank Marketing*, 37 (4), pp. 1062–1079.

Maignan, I. & Ferrell, O. C. (2004). Corporate Social Responsibility and Marketing: An Integrative Framework. *Journal of the Academy of Marketing Science*, 32 (1), pp. 3–19.

Marin, L., Ruiz, S. & Rubio, A. (2009). The Role of Identity Salience in the Effects of Corporate Social Responsibility on Consumer Behavior. *Journal of Business Ethics*, 84 (1), pp. 65–78.

Mayntz, R. (1967). Modellkonstruktion: Ansatz, Typen und Zweck. In *Formalisierte Modelle in der Soziologie* (pp. 111–31). Luchterhand.

Mazutis, D. D. & Slawinski, N. (2015). Reconnecting Business and Society: Perceptions of Authenticity in Corporate Social Responsibility. *Journal of Business Ethics*, 131 (1), pp. 137–150.

McEwen, W. (2004). Why Satisfaction Isn't Satisfying. *Gallup Management Journal Online*, November 11.

Mcshane, L. & Cunningham, P. (2012). To Thine Own Self Be True? Employees' Judgments of the Authenticity of Their Organization's Corporate Social Responsibility Program. *Journal of Business Ethics*, 108 (1), pp. 81–100.

Menon, S. & Kahn, B. E. (2003). Corporate Sponsorships of Philanthropic Activities: When Do They Impact Perception of Sponsor Brand?. *Journal of Consumer Psychology*, 13 (3), pp. 316–327.

Moehl, S. & Friedman, B. A. (2022). Consumer Perceived Authenticity of Organizational Corporate Social Responsibility (CSR) Statements: A Test of Attribution Theory. *Social Responsibility Journal*, 18 (4), pp. 875–893.

Mohr, L. A. & Webb, D. J. (2005). The Effects of Corporate Social Responsibility and Price on Consumer Responses. *The Journal of Consumer Affairs*, 39 (1 Summer 2005), pp. 121–147.

Morhart, F., Malär, L., Guèvremont, A., Girardin, F. & Grohmann, B. (2015). Brand Authenticity: An Integrative Framework and Measurement Scale. *Journal of Consumer Psychology*, 25 (2), pp. 200–218.

Moulard, J. G., Raggio, R. D. & Folse, J. A. G. (2021). Disentangling the Meanings of Brand Authenticity: The Entity-Referent Correspondence Framework of Authenticity. *Journal of the Academy of Marketing Science*, 49 (1), pp. 96–118.

Mulaessa, N. & Wang, H. (2017). The Effect of Corporate Social Responsibility (CSR) Activities on Consumers Purchase Intention in China: Mediating Role of Consumer Support for Responsible Business. *International Journal of Marketing Studies*, 9 (1), p. 73.

Nan, X. & Heo, K. (2007). Consumer Responses to Corporate Social Responsibility (CSR) Initiatives: Examining the Role of Brand-Cause Fit in Cause-Related Marketing. *Journal of Advertising*, 36 (2), pp. 63–74.

Nardella, G., Brammer, S. & Surdu, I. (2020). Shame on Who? The Effects of Corporate Irresponsibility and Social Performance on Organizational Reputation. *British Journal of Management*, 31 (1), pp. 5–23.

Park, J., Lee, H. & Kim, C. (2014). Corporate Social Responsibilities, Consumer Trust and Corporate Reputation: South Korean Consumers' Perspectives. *Journal of Business Research*, 67 (3), pp. 295–302.

Pérez, A. (2019). Building a Theoretical Framework of Message Authenticity in CSR Communication. *Corporate Communications: An International Journal*, 24 (2), pp. 334–350.

Perfors, A., Tenenbaum, J. B., Griffiths, T. L. & Xu, F. (2011). A Tutorial Introduction to Bayesian Models of Cognitive Development. *Cognition*, 120 (3), pp. 302–321.

Popper, K. R. (1959). *The Logic of Scientific discovery*. The Logic of Scientific Discovery. Basic Books.

Porter, M. & Kramer, M. (2007). Strategy and Society: The Link Between Competitive Advantage and Corporate Social Responsibility. *Harvard Business Review*, 84, pp. 78–92, 163.

Porter, M. & Kramer, M. (2011). The Big Idea: Creating Shared Value. How to Reinvent Capitalism – and Unleash a Wave of Innovation and Growth. *Harvard Business Review*, 89 pp. 62–77.

Price, L. L., Arnould, E. J. & Tierney, P. (1995). Going to Extremes: Managing Service Encounters and Assessing Provider Performance. *Journal of Marketing*, 59 (2), p. 83.

Ranfagni, S. & Guercini, S. (2016). *Beyond Appearances: The Hidden Meanings of Sustainable Luxury* (pp. 51–72).

Rodriguez-Gomez, S., Arco-Castro, M. L., Lopez-Perez, M. V. & Rodríguez-Ariza, L. (2020). Where Does CSR Come from and Where Does It Go? A Review of the State of the Art. *Administrative Sciences*, 10 (3), p. 60.

Sampaio, A. R., Thomas, R. & Font, X. (2012). Why Are Some Engaged and Not Others? Explaining Environmental Engagement among Small Firms in Tourism. *International Journal of Tourism Research*, 14 (3), pp. 235–249.

Saunders, M., Lewis, P. & Thornhill, A. (2014). *Research Methods for Business Students*. Pearson Education.

Schaefer, A. D. & Pettijohn, C. E. (2006). The Relevance of Authenticity in Personal Selling: Is Genuineness an Asset or Liability?. *Journal of Marketing Theory and Practice*, 14 (1), pp. 25–35.

Schaefer, S. D., Terlutter, R. & Diehl, S. (2019). Is My Company Really Doing Good? Factors Influencing Employees' Evaluation of the Authenticity of Their Company's Corporate Social Responsibility Engagement. *Journal of Business Research*, 101, pp. 128–143.

Scherer, A. G. & Palazzo, G. (2011). The New Political Role of Business in a Globalized World: A Review of a New Perspective on CSR and its Implications for the Firm, Governance, and Democracy. *Journal of Management Studies*, 48 (4), pp. 899–931.

Sen, S. & Bhattacharya, C. B. (2001). Does Doing Good Always Lead to Doing Better? Consumer Reactions to Corporate Social Responsibility. *Journal of Marketing Research (JMR)*, 38 (2), pp. 225–243.

Sen, S., Bhattacharya, C. B. & Korschun, D. (2006). The Role of Corporate Social Responsibility in Strengthening Multiple Stakeholder Relationships: A Field Experiment. *Journal of the Academy of Marketing Science*, 34 (2), pp. 158–166.

Skilton, P. F. & Purdy, J. M. (2017). Authenticity, Power, and Pluralism: A Framework for Understanding Stakeholder Evaluations of Corporate Social Responsibility Activities. *Business Ethics Quarterly*, 27 (1), pp. 99–123.

Speed, R. & Thompson, P. (2000). Determinants of Sports Sponsorship Response. *Journal of the Academy of Marketing Science*, 28 (2), pp. 226–238.

Statista (2022). *Fast Fashion: Filialisten weltweit und in Deutschland.* https://www.statista.de

Tajfel, H. & Turner, J. C. (1979). An Integrative Theory of Intergroup Conflict. *Organizational Identity: A Reader*, 56 (65).

Turner, J. C., Oakes, P. J., Haslam, S. A. & Mcgarty, C. (1994). Self and Collective: Cognition and Social Context. *Personality and Social Psychology Bulletin*, 20 (5), pp. 454–463.

Uniqlo. (2022b). *Uniqlo's Support to Refugees and Others Forced from Home.* https://www.uniqlo.com/jp/en/contents/sustainability/society/refugees/

Van Marrewijk, M. (2003). Concepts and Definitions of CSR and Corporate Sustainability: Between Agency and Communion. *Journal of Business Ethics*, 44 (2), pp. 95–105.

van Rekom, J., Go, F. M. & Calter, D. M. (2014). Communicating a Company's Positive Impact on Society—Can Plausible Explanations Secure Authenticity?. *Journal of Business Research*, 67 (9), pp. 1831–1838.

Vilanova, M., Lozano, J. M. & Arenas, D. (2009). Exploring the Nature of the Relationship Between CSR and Competitiveness. *Journal of Business Ethics*, 87 (S1), pp. 57–69.

Wagner, T., Lutz, R. & Weitz, B. (2009). Corporate Hypocrisy: Overcoming the Threat of Inconsistent Corporate Social Responsibility Perceptions. *Journal of Marketing American Marketing Association ISSN*, 73 pp. 77–91.

Wang, H., Gibson, C. & Zander, U. (2020). Editors' Comments: Is Research on Corporate Social Responsibility Undertheorized? *Academy of Management Briarcliff Manor,* NY. 45, pp. 1–6.

Williams, O. (2014). CSR: Will It Change the World? – Hope for the Future: An Emerging Logic in Business Practice. *Journal of Corporate Citizenship*, 2014.

Yeomans, M. (2018). *Marketers Beware: Gen Z Wants Action, Not Flashy Campaigns*. Reuters Events Sustainable Business.

Yoo, D. & Lee, J. (2018). The Effects of Corporate Social Responsibility (CSR) Fit and CSR Consistency on Company Evaluation: The Role of CSR Support. *Sustainability*, 10 (8), pp. 2956.

Zhu, L., He, Y., Chen, Q. & Hu, M. (2017). It's the Thought That Counts: The Effects of Construal Level Priming and Donation Proximity on Consumer Response to Donation Framing. *Journal of Business Research*, 76, pp. 44–51.

Martina Chalupová, Jan Voráček and František Smrčka

3. Urgent Information Exchange System to Support Internationalisation in Higher Education Institutions

Abstract: Internationalisation belongs among the key components of the activities of higher education institutions (HEIs). Management of international processes and activities requires sophisticated and interconnected information system. The aim of the chapter is to present a proposal of a system for urgent information exchange, built on the system diagram presenting the most important variables and relations within the HEIs internationalisation, including key stakeholders. The model represents a decision-support tool that facilitates the inclusion of the processes that reflect internationalisation governance structures and the theory of situation awareness into the existing university administration. The proposed system for urgent information exchange is designed using Unified Process (UP) methodology, a generic process for Unified Modelling Language (UML). The chapter presents suitable information technologies such as Firebase Cloud Messaging for sending information from the information system to the mobile application and APIs for connecting applications to the information system.

Keywords: Internationalisation, urgent information exchange system, conceptual modelling, UML, UP

3.1. Introduction

Internationalisation has become one of the central themes of the debate on the future of higher education institutions (HEIs) (Altbach, 2016; Brooks & Walters, 2013; Gacel-Ávila, 2005). Over the years, in response to increasing geopolitical and economic imperatives, it has grown significantly from a marginal point of interest to a fundamental factor of the universities and colleges (Egron-Polak & Hudson, 2014; Gao et al., 2015; Wihlborg &Robson, 2018). As a mass phenomenon, the international dimension has shifted from a reactive to a pro-active strategic issue (De Wit, 2011). The HE internationalisation concept is included in various levels of policy frameworks, representing a complex of issues and policies with different approaches and strategies in constantly changing contexts within the knowledge-based economy (Cheng et al., 2017; Knight & de Wit, 2018). One of the most used definitions describes the internationalisation as a process that *"integrates an international, intercultural, or global dimension into the purpose, functions or delivery of post-secondary education"* (Knight, 2008,

p. 21). As Qiang (2003) emphasised, it is a dynamic process that covers a wide range of dimensions and approaches, not a set of detached activities. Results of the European Universities Initiative survey, which analysed data from 219 HEIs from 34 systems across Europe, show that internationalisation has been a strategic issue at most institutions for quite a while: more than half of respondents have 10% or more international students (Claeys-Kulik et al., 2020).

The concept of internationalisation is strongly anchored in institutional mission statements, policies and strategies, including national policy frameworks; it represents a complex of issues and policies with different approaches and strategies in constantly changing contexts (Knight & de Wit, 2018). Wihlborg & Robson (2018) call for readjustment of research approaches of the HEIs' international activities, becoming more cross-disciplinary and transversal to be able to address various types of modern challenges. De Wit and Hunter (2015) focused on the future of internationalisation of higher education in Europe and suggested that the main challenges are international strategic partnerships and increasing outgoing student mobility, which remains a crucial activity of institutional and regional policies in the EU. Other forms, such as academic programmes (i.e., cross-cultural training, exchange programmes, visiting lectures, joint/double degree programs), collaboration on the research projects or extra-curricular activities, such as students' associations and external relations (domestic and cross-border), help build the complex international activities (Maringe & Foskett, 2010).

In order to manage such complex and dynamic processes related to international activities and processes, institutional leaders should include additional governing interconnected structures and systems, protecting their students and academics or staff from impacts of unpredictable, turbulent, and multifaceted changes (Chalupová et al., 2020). We believe that using a system for urgent information exchange for international mobilities at universities is still relatively scarce. Its application range (being user-friendly and architecturally scalable) may be considered as extensive, providing an individual or a team with information support.

3.2. Situation Awareness

One of the most applicable situation awareness definitions sees it as *"the perception of the elements in the environment within a volume of time and space, the comprehension of their meaning and the projection of their status in the near future"* (Endsley, 1995). It may be thought of as a non-trivial transformation, converting continuously acquired information into partial decisions, especially at the tactical and strategic levels of management (Voráček & Přibyl, 2020). From an organisational point of view, it therefore affects processes with a period of weeks to months. Using this inertia, the conversion of perceived or measured facts into concrete actions cannot be purely reflexive or predictive, but requires broader contextual knowledge, combining static and dynamic qualitative and quantitative aspects of the decision. Creating and updating of situational awareness must therefore continuously integrate the acquired data into appropriate information and eventually knowledge frameworks (Voráček et al., 2021). In general, lack of situational awareness is considered one of the main sources of error caused by the human factor.

Situational awareness is characterised as a sequence of the following three basic activities, leading to eventual decisions and their implementation (Endsley & Garland, 2000):

(a) perception of the environment in the context of space and time;
(b) understanding the meaning of continuously acquired information;
(c) projecting this knowledge into the future.

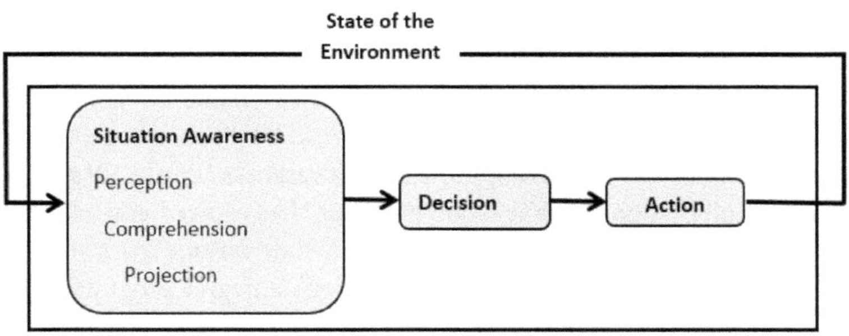

Figure 3.1: Simplified Model of Situation Awareness, Source: Endsley, 2012, p. 557, own adjustment

Aspects of situational awareness have been addressed within the military context (Mittrick et al., 2018; Murray et al., 2010; Strater et al., 2001), emergency systems (Arendtsen et al., 2016), or healthcare systems (Alhaider et al., 2018; Qazi et al., 2020). In this context, recent Joint Communication to the European Parliament, the European Parliament, the European Council, the Economic and Social Committee and the Committee of the Regions JOIN2020/8 – Combating Misinformation on COVID-19 – Truths and Myths (European Union, 2020) can be mentioned. Its goal is a closer cooperation between the EU states in the field of sharing information and knowledge on epidemiological situation. The initial lack of information has led to the creation and dissemination of incomplete and inaccurate information, potentially leading to erroneous decisions at all levels of management.

3.3. Factors Affecting HEI Internationalisation

When considering international activities, HEI management must take into account a wide range of factors, starting at the macro-level (political, cultural, social, technological, economic factors), and continuing with mezzo factors (connected with regional conditions) as well as the inner context (Cairns, 2019; Curaj et al., 2018; Van Mol & Timmermann, 2014). To manage complex processes connected with internationalisation, HEI management should prepare additional structures and processes to be able to guide, inform and support their incoming and outgoing students and academics/staff to minimise impacts of unpredictable and complex events and changes, such as terrorist attacks (Dostál et al., 2018), local crises and conflicts (Cervantes-Duarte & Fernández-Cano, 2016), protectionism or various forms of inequalities (Choudaha, 2017) or the health crises, such as COVID-19 pandemic (Wang et al., 2020; Huang et al., 2022). It is certain that HEI internationalisation and various types of external risks can be managed with the methods similar to those used for business processes (Al-Zoubi et al., 2018). The benefits might include improvement in the management of the internationalisation process, better rationale for decisions, more realistic planning and increased risk and opportunities awareness (Polak, 2018).

The HEIs internationalisation scope in the EU has evolved considerably (de Wit & Hunter, 2015). The most frequent forms include various types of academic programmes (exchange programmes or joint/double degree programs, lectures from visiting academics, cross-cultural training, etc.), research collaboration, or extra-curricular activities, such as students' associations (domestic and cross-border) (Altbach et al., 2006; Maringe & Foskett, 2010). Research that focused on the EU showed that internationalisation is considered to be a strategic element at most institutions (Claeys-Kulik et al., 2020): almost 90% of HEIs are engaging in the students' credit mobility, EU research projects and staff mobility, 80% of the respondents aim to attract international degree students, and about three-quarters of respondents collaborate on joint degree programmes and bilateral research activities. HEIs in Europe act within the European Higher Education Area (EHEA), which was established in 2010 as a part of the Bologna Process; Erasmus+ represents the EU's key programme to support education, training, youth and sport. More than 10 million people have participated in Erasmus+ over the last three decades.

The context of European higher education is marked by accelerating changes. Curaj et al. (2018) identified several challenges that should not be ignored; regarding technological environment, authors mention the digital revolution, as the digitalisation transformed into a basic social necessity. Political factors, such as the rise of populist ideologies, weakening consensus on political principles (Choudaha, 2017), as well as increase in extremism and terrorist attacks (Chalupová et al., 2017; Dostál et al. 2018) have a broad impact on the HE internationalisation. Economic and social factors that bear on HE policies include emerging protectionism and divergent approach to globalism, population ageing (growing demographic decline), the ongoing refugee crisis, military conflicts, growing inequalities and youth unemployment (Curaj et al., 2018; Roy et al., 2019). Widely accepted Model of Coordination in Higher Education (Clark's Triangle) attempts to explain the interplay of factors that have an impact on HEIs performance (Salazar & Leighy, 2013). The dynamic model that incorporates the state (various levels of government), market and the academia (colleges and universities collectively) presents a flexible framework that enables the study of evolving relationships among the actors/stakeholders in the higher education system. Central to the model are the concepts of knowledge, beliefs and authority (Maggio, 2013). Several authors (Brennan, 2010; Enders & de Weert, 2009; Hermanowicz, 2018) have exposed some insufficiencies in the model in connection with the growing number of networks between the HEIs, rising importance of the economic logic in the educational space, and the influence of the non-academic stakeholders. According to Qiang (2003), who applied this model for coordination of higher education in an international context, specific attention should be paid to the interplay of various international and national forces and actors in the government, education and private sector.

3.4. Student Mobility – The System Dynamics

The European HEIs operate within the European Higher Education Area (EHEA), launched in 2010 as an integral part of the Bologna Process, to build coherence among Europe's higher education systems (EHEA, 2020). The EU's cornerstone programme to support education, training, youth and sport in Europe is Erasmus+ with 34 participating Programme Countries. Over the last three decades, more than 10 million people have already participated in it. In May 2018, the European Commission proposed to double the Programme's budget to €30 billion for the next 7-year period, which, among all, should aim to enhance mobility and cooperation in EU and with the rest of the world (European Commission, 2018). Several initiatives (such as the European Universities initiative), launched by the

European Commission, are helping build the European Education Area by 2025, which will reinforce learning, teaching and training mobility for students and staff in higher education (European Commission, 2018).

At the national level, there are government units with an active role in the international dimension of the HEIs – primarily a ministry of education and the accreditation bodies – but also other authorities involved in the foreign affairs, economic and regional development, business and trade, science and technology or culture (Capano, 2008; Castro et al., 2015). The higher education sector involves diverse types of HEIs, as well as the research and discipline groups, the professional associations and other advocacy or issue groups. It also includes internal stakeholders such as students, personnel (academics and administrators) and institutional leaders (Marshall, 2018; Ketunen, 2014). The private sector is much broader, with the businesses and organisations with varied international interests (Qiang, 2003). HEI's exposure to a range of stakeholders, together with the pressure for achieving higher productivity, economic performance and market principles in the management (Howels et al., 2014), has emphasised the importance of leadership to balance institutional logics in times of uncertainty, caused by the various multifaceted changes in the global environment.

According to Cairns (2019), student mobility within the EU provides measurements of programmatic success to stakeholders and policymakers. HEIs are responsible for the number of outgoing students with significant differences between approaches of individual universities. Presented in 2018, the current vision of the European Commission for the European Education Area by 2025 is envisioning mobility possibilities for everybody, without borders. Erasmus+ is a driving force by boosting student mobility and stimulating long-term transnational alliances of HEIs (European Commission, 2018).

Many authors have studied the drivers and barriers of student mobility. According to Beine et al. (2014), completed student mobility may ease access to the labour market. Van Mol and Timmerman (2014) have examined student mobility determinants according to the students´ personal motivations. Student mobility seems to be driven by a search for the personal growth, a possible improvement of employability and new experiences (Heublein et al., 2008; Rosenmund et al., 2012). Also, interest in foreign cultures and countries could become a motivating factor (King & Ruiz-Gelices, 2003). Learning English might be a positive factor among participating students (González et al., 2011; Tosi et al., 2019). On the other side, this could be a powerful barrier, mostly for students who are not proficient in foreign languages (Findlay et al., 2006). A separation from the family and friends appears to be another obstacle, as well as insufficient financial resources for the participation (Beerkens et al., 2016). De Wit and Hunter (2015) highlight, among others, barriers such as: bureaucratic difficulties, lack of involvement and remuneration of staff in educational establishments, or insufficient links between educational institutions and policies at national and transnational levels. Van Mol (2013) presented the system of factors with the major influence on student mobility, in which students' personal motivations are framed with the global context and macro-environment of the students' home country.

Researches by Pyvis and Chapman (2007) and Tran (2016) identify positional and transformative investments as two main factors influencing students' decision to undertake international education. Positional motivation turns out to be pragmatic and subsidiary. It indicates the way in which international education is seen as a means to enable students to achieve higher social status or employment opportunity, as previously discussed, which help them create a competitive advantage for their life. Students with transformative investment, however, see international education as providing them with the opportunity to enhance their cultural, personal and professional perspective. Other authors have advanced the Pyvis & Chapman´s study (e. g. Findlay, 2011; Holloway et al., 2012; Wadhwa, 2018). Robertson et al. (2011) shifted the study by explaining the interlocked positional and transformative stimulus and results of gaining international education including migration opportunities, personal enrichment, career advancement and new views on work and life.

Choudaha (2017) has divided changes in international student mobility into three overlapping "waves", spreading over between 1999–2020, with the major events and trends in international politics and economics as a cornerstone. The first two waves coincided with terrorist attacks on the USA in 2001 and the global financial recession, which triggered financial motivations for recruiting international students. The third one was shaped by BREXIT, and it is apparent that the COVID-19 pandemic had an enormous impact on the recent forms of HEIs internationalisation (Huang et al., 2022; Hunter et al., 2022; Farnell et al., 2021).

3.5. Methodology

Implementations of high-level organisational policies and strategies result in complex, dynamic, heavily interconnected systems. Nontrivial problems connected with internationalisation, accompanied by a considerable portion of human-related soft factors, uncertainty, nonlinearity, and parametric nonstationarity, are impossible to be solved purely formally (Chalupová et al.,

2020). Modern representational and computational techniques may facilitate situation and process modelling in such naturally ambiguous environments (Bui, 2020). Because of the qualitative and time-varying nature of the studied phenomenon, we based our outcomes on theoretical foundations and methods from systems thinking and organisational learning. According to Senge (1990), modern management must be holistic and systemic, including large involvement of human-related factors, such as personal mastery, mental models, shared vision, and team learning.

As the basics for the design of the innovative urgent information exchange system, we have decided to present a system diagram of internationalisation with situation awareness activities. It helped identify key performance subsystems and factors, representing an aggregate overview of qualitative dynamics (Ferrario et al., 2016). The UP (Unified Process), shortened form of the USDP (Unified Software Development Process), methodology was then used to design a system for urgent information exchange. It represents a generic process for UML – Unified Modeling Language, an open methodology that can be adapted to the scope of any project. It must be tailored to the goals and conditions of a given development, i. e. standards, tools, templates etc. (Smrčka et al., 2022). The Unified Process (UP) presents controlled requirements and use cases, providing risk management and the basis of the architecture, an iterative and incremental process for developing SW products. The UP is divided into iterations, each of which goes through generic work processes: requirements definition, analysis, design, implementation, testing, iteration in the UP (Schmuller, 2001).

The UML language provides a visual syntax that can be used to build models. UML provides a standard procedure for writing system designs, including conceptual components such as business processes and system functions, as well as concrete components such as programming language commands, database schemas, and reusable software components. UML can model or document any information system virtually. The UML deployment diagram was chosen to represent the urgent system. A deployment diagram describes the placement of functional units (components) on the computational nodes of an information system. The deployment diagram is intended for the implementation phase. Its main purpose is to show the relationships between the parts of the system as they appear at the time of actual execution. The deployment diagram shows the distribution of the individual SW components on HW resources and their cooperation, the distribution of HW and SW resources in the sites, the topology of the networks used, and the types and use of communication resources (Bruckner, 2012).

3.6. Design of an Urgent Information Exchange System Supporting HEI Internationalisation

Achieved results are represented in a graphic format. The system diagram in Figure 3.2 presents the most important variables and relations within internationalisation, including key stakeholders (*governmental bodies, university board, international partnership network, management of internationalisation, services* – international departments, and *students*). It assumes an existing interconnected *management system,* which allows risk management analysis. The proposed system diagram supports and enhances *situation awareness*. The key relations are marked with bolded arrows.

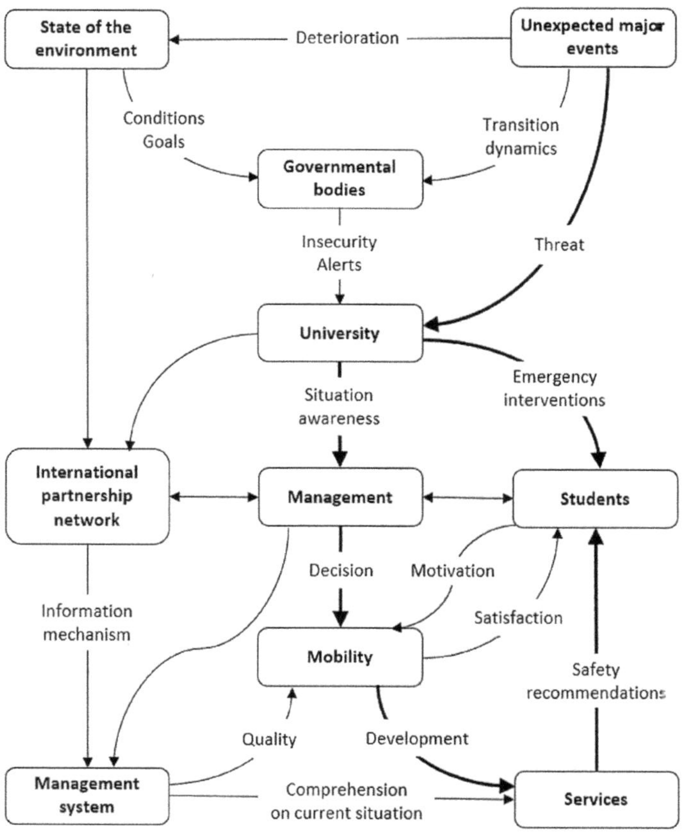

Figure 3.2: System diagram of the proposed mobility management system

The upper part of this diagram shows two directions, how *unexpected major events* (e. g. military conflict, natural disasters, terrorism) can affect university and their students. Their pervasive, indirect, evolutionary perception through other environmental factors (*state of the environment*) have an effect on conditions and goals that are being introduced by the governmental bodies (such as Ministry of Education or Ministry of Foreign Affairs). Generally, anticipable dynamics may be a relative advantage of this input, giving the *university* board and *management of the internationalisation* time for strategic planning of adequate resilience. The second entry of consequences of *unexpected events*, as seen in Figure 3.2 in the top right part, may be direct and fast, representing a direct *threat* and demonstrating the need for the urgent information exchange system. In this case, immediate reactions, according to pre-prepared scenarios, must be applied in close cooperation with the *international partnership network*. It is obvious that no emergency plan can accurately reflect reality, but it can effectively decrease negative effects when combined with consistently used risk management measures. In the right lower quadrant of Figure 3.2, there are additional activities with elementary dynamics shown. These are provided together with standard *mobility*-related information by a *services* unit, responsible for international relations. Disregarding particular details, the primary goal of this department is to motivate *students* to travel and to provide them with the *safety recommendations*.

The basis of the proposed system for urgent information exchange is the inner block (see Figure 3.3). The inner side contains the REST API for communication with the database, the generation of the security token JWT (JSON Web Token), and methods for inserting and receiving urgent information (Firebase Cloud Messaging, 2021). REST (Representational State Transfer) is an API (Application Programming Interface) architecture that allows you to access data in a database. The REST API uses the web app and the mobile app to store and manage data in the database. JWT is a method to securely exchange information between two parties. In our design, it is used for REST API security. Urgent information can be entered via the web app or mobile app. The inner block sends urgent information to the Fire Base using the App method. FireBase is a Google's mobile platform that allows sending information in the form of a notification to all mobile phones that have their Mobile App registered in the Fire Base application (Heryandi, 2018). Users (managers) work with the system by designing either a web app or a mobile app on their mobile phone. The mobile phone assumes an Android operating system. HTTP is a protocol for retrieving resources such as HTML documents. It is the basis of all data exchange on the web and it is a client-server protocol, i.e. requests are initiated by the recipient, usually the web browser.

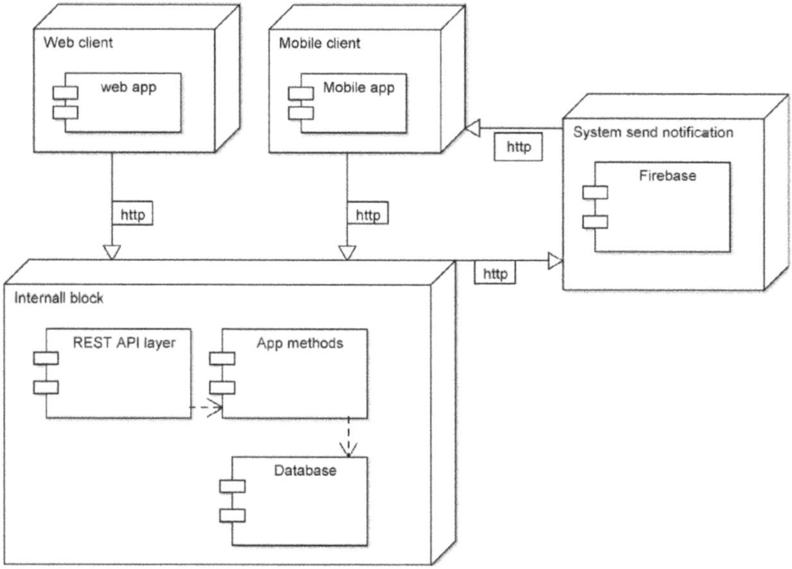

Figure 3.3: Deployment diagram of a system for the exchange of urgent information in case of unexpected events

Figure 3.4 illustrates the design of a system for the exchange of urgent information in case of unexpected events. The practical operation of the urgent information exchange system is shown in Figure 3.5. A student on his/her mobility downloads an app with the emergency system to his/her mobile phone (tablet). Suppose it is necessary to inform students in real time about an unexpected event with major impact on their mobility. In that case, the management responsible for international relations enter information into the information system, containing a basic description of the problem and also more detailed description. The basic information will appear on the student's mobile phone in the form of a notification. More detailed information is provided to the students using the application. The communication between the information system and the mobile application is bidirectional so that the students can send back their requests.

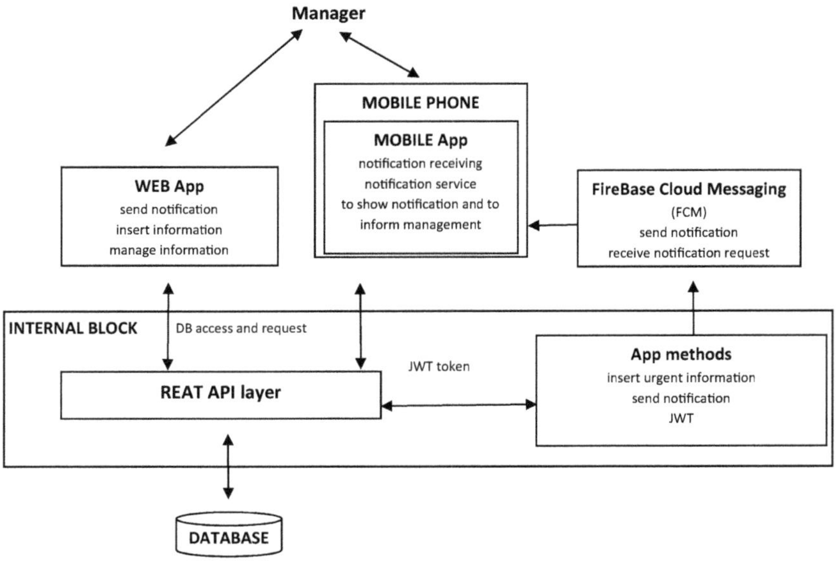

Figure 3.4: Design of a system for the exchange of urgent information in case of unexpected events

The created IT solution, i.e., a system with an application that uses IT technologies (such as real-time notifications and mobile applications), minimizes time delays in the form of real-time notifications. The proposed system includes an API interface to connect other external entities such as the Ministry of Foreign Affairs (*Connected entities*). Communication with these entities is one-way, i.e. students only receive urgent information and alerts about, for example, impending natural disasters (earthquakes, floods), political instability, strikes, and so on.

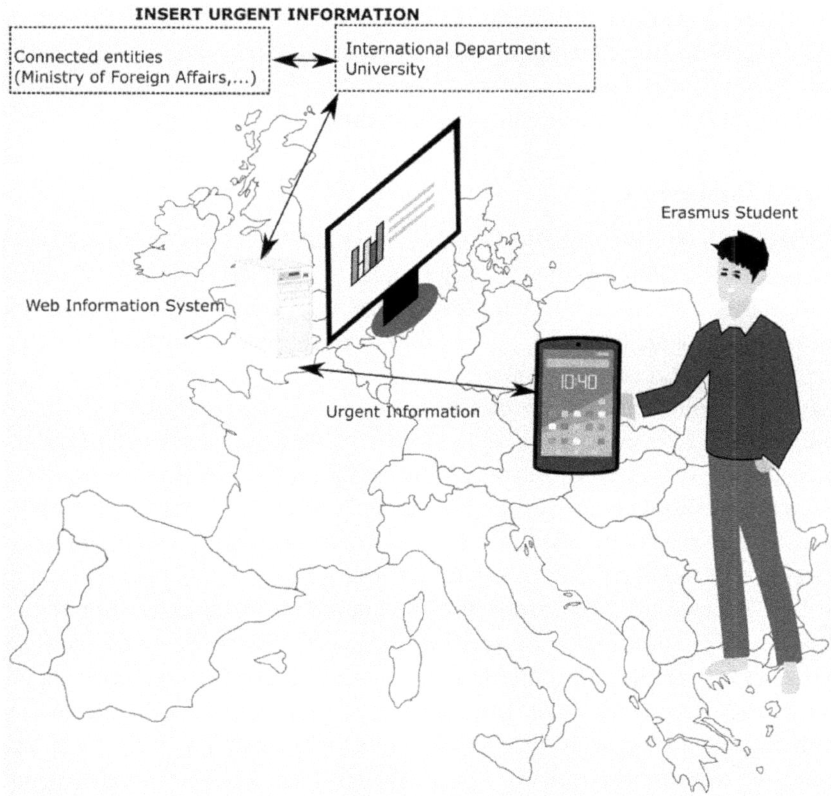

Figure 3.5: Practical operation of the urgent information exchange system

Figure 3.5 shows that the information, including possible urgent information, is entered into the system by the university before sending the student on a mobility. These pre-prepared notifications need to be updated before their use. The proposed system has an API and therefore, it is possible for other entities, such as the Ministry of Foreign Affairs, to connect to the system. The university international department will fill in the student's information, including country and place of residence, before each departure. The basic information about the student will be imported from the university's information system (again, a REST API). The student will install an app on his/her mobile phone that will allow two-way communication with the information system. That means that the student will receive urgent information and be able to ask questions. The administration of the system, i.e., the management of the urgent information, will be the responsibility of the designated staff member of the university's international department. It will also be possible to exchange information from other entities, such as partner HEIs (their international departments).

3.7. Conclusion

International student mobility remains one of the main pillars of HEIs internationalisation, playing a major role in the development of global competencies of students and academics. Processes affecting mobilities should meet requirements of clarity, accessibility, and efficiency. Our proposal of the urgent information exchange system falls into the category of prevention. Such activities require additional resources, assuming that other performance drivers and enablers remain on the base level. In a stable world, without unexpected transformative events, additional processes logically cause security overhead. However, we would argue that an unprepared university would face not only a considerable drop of mobile students but it would also lose its own performance because of mandatory ad-hoc recovery solutions.

Our main recommendations for the mobilities include: (i) universities should classify destination countries according to the well-defined risks, (ii) systematically prepare outgoing students to be able to react to unexpected major events, (iii) together with international partners, prepare and test an information exchange system that would secure interconnectivity, flexibility and provide real-time, well addressed information. The proposed system must constantly respond to changing conditions, and unpredictable, multifaceted challenges with major impact in the environment and emerging new threats. For this reason, the system is to be perceived as an open one that continuously adapts to the current situation in the world. The chapter proposes suitable information technologies using which the urgent system can be programmed.

Our further research will be focused on the importance of trust in the HEIs' international networking as an important element within the information exchange and a determinant of success and development of sustainable partnerships.

References

Alhaider, A. A., Lau, N., Davenport, P. B., Morris, M. K. & Tuck, C. (2018). Distributed Situation Awareness in Patient Flow Management: An Admission Case Study. *Proceedings of the Human Factors and Ergonomics Society Annual Meeting*, 62, pp. 563–567.

Al-Zoubi, A., Polak, M. & Savior, R. (2018). A Mature Institutional Management Model of Internationalisation in MENA Universities. *Journal of Education and Human Development*. 9 (3), pp. 28–38. https://doi.org/10.15640/jehd.v7n3a4

Altbach, P. G. (2016). *Global Perspectives on Higher Education*. Johns Hopkins University Press.

Altbach, P. G., Reisberg, L. & Rumbley, L. E. (2009) *Trends in Global Higher Education: Tracking an Academic Revolution*. Boston College Center for International Higher Education.

Arendtsen, B., Baker, S., Bertels, M., Brookes, D., Catherwood, D., Christiansen, K., Cuypers, W., Edgar, G., Krawczynska, S., Maes, V., Sallis, G., Stegienko, K., Craybex, G., Vastmans, J., Vorenkamp, F., Weewer, R. & Wenarski, G. (2016). Firemind: Trialling a New Tool for Training Fire and Rescue Service Decision-Making. *International Fire Professional Journal*, pp. 4–17.

Beerkens, M., Souto-Otero, M., de Wit, H. & Huisman, J. (2016). Similar Students and Different Countries? An Analysis of the Barriers and Drivers for Erasmus Participation in Seven Countries. *Journal of Studies in International Education*, 20 (2), pp. 184–204.

Beine, M., Noël, R. & Ragot, L. (2014). Determinants of the International Mobility of Students. *Economics of Education Review*, 41, I. C, pp. 40–54.

Brennan, J. (2010). Burton Clark's The Higher Education System: Academic Organization in Cross-National Perspective. *London Review of Education*, 8 (3), pp. 229–237.

Brooks, R. & Walters, J. (2013). *Student Mobilities, Migration and the Internationalization of Higher Education*. Palgrave Macmillan.

Bruckner, T. (2012). *Creating Information Systems: Principles, Methodologies, Architectures*. Grada, Management in the Information Society.

Bui, H. T. M. (2020). From the Fifth Discipline to the New Revolution: What We Have Learnt from Senge's Ideas Over the Last Three Decades. *The Learning Organization*, 27 (6), pp. 489–498.

Cairns, D. (2019). Researching Social Inclusion in Student Mobility: Methodological Strategies in Studying the Erasmus Programme. *International Journal of Research & Method in Education*, 42 (2), pp. 137–147.

Capano, G. (2008). Looking for Serendipity: The Problematical Reform of Government Within Italy's Universities. *Higher Education*, 55 (4), pp. 491–504.

Castro, R., Rosa, M. J. & Pinho, C. (2015). A Model for Stakeholders' Influence on Internationalization. *Journal of Studies in International Education*, 19 (2), pp. 160–181.

Cervantes-Duarte, L. & Fernández-Cano, A. (2016). Impact of Armed Conflicts on Education and Educational Agents: A Multivocal Review. *Revista Electrónica Educare*, 20 (3), pp. 1–24.

Chalupová, M., Dostál, J., Černá, M. & Prokop, M. (2017). Terrorist Attacks in the EU and their Impact on Short-Term Student Mobilities – Case of International Business Weeks Network. *Turkish Online Journal of Educational Technology, 16* (Spec. Issue for INTE 2017), pp. 82–90.

Chalupová, M., Voráček, J. & Činčalová, S. (2020). Anti-Terrorism Policy for International Students' Mobility: A Conceptual Model. In *15th International Forum on Knowledge Asset Dynamics Proceedings*, University of Basilicata, pp. 855–99.

Cheng, M., Kitigawa, F. & Osborne, M. (2017). The Evolution of Internationalisation strategy: a case study of the University of Nottingham. *International Journal of Knowledge-Based Development*, 8 (3).

Choudaha, R. (2017). Three Waves of International Student Mobility (1999–2020). *Studies in Higher Education*, 45 (5), pp. 1–8.

Claeys-Kulik, Jørgensen, Stöber et al. (2020). International Strategic Institutional Partnerships and the European Universities Initiative, Results of the EUA survey. [Online, April 10, 2023], https://eua.eu/resources/publications/925:international-strategic-institutional-partnerships-and-the-european-universities-initiative.html.

Curaj, A., Deca, L. & Priciope, R. (2018). Twenty Years of Bologna and a Decade of EHEA: What's Next? In A. Curaj, L. Deca & R. Priciope (Eds.), *European Higher Education Area: The Impact of Past and Future Policies* (pp. 1–11). Springer International Publishing.

De Wit, H. (2011). Globalisation and Internationalisation of Higher Education. *Revista de Universidad y Sociedad del Conocimiento (RUSC)*, 8 (2), pp. 241–248.

De Wit, H. & Hunter, F. (2015). Understanding Internationalisation of Higher Education in the European Context. In Hans de Wit, Fiona Hunter, Laura Hunter and Eva Egron-Polak (Eds.), *Internationalisation in Higher Education. A study for the European Parliament's Committee on Culture and Education* (pp. 411–58). European Union Publications Office, ((2015)540370). http://www.europarl.europa.eu/thinktank/en/document.html?reference=IPOL_STU

Dostál, J., Chalupová, M., Černá, M. & Prokop, M. (2018). International Terrorism as a Threat to Student Mobility. *On the Horizon*, 26 (2), pp. 91–102.

Egron-Polak, E. & Hudson, R. (2014). *Internationalization of Higher Education: Growing Expectations, Fundamental Values.* IAU 4th Global Survey. [Online, March 27, 2023], https://www.iau-aiu.net/Global-survey-on-Internationalization

EHEA (2020). *Rome Ministerial Communiqué,* [Online, April 10, 2023], https://www.ehea.info/Upload/Rome_Ministerial_Communique.pdf

Enders, J. & de Weert, E. (2009). *The Changing Face of Academic Life: Analytical and Comparative Perspectives.* Palgrave Macmillan.

Endsley, M. R. (1995). Toward a Theory of Situation Awareness in Dynamic Systems. *Human Factors Journal and Ergonomics Society*, 37, pp. 32–64.

Endsley, M. R. & Garland, D. J. (Eds.) (2000). *Situation Awareness Analysis and Measurement* (1st ed.). CRC Press.

Endsley, M. R. (2012). Situation Awareness. In G. Salvendy (Ed.), *Handbook of Human Factors and Ergonomics* (4th ed., pp. 553–568). Wiley & Sons.

European Commission (2018). *Erasmus+ Annual Report 2018, European Union.* [Online, March 17, 2023], https://op.europa.eu/en/publication-detail/-/publication/

European Union (2020). *EUR-Lex – 52020JC0008 – EN – EUR-Lex.* [Online, March 7, 2023], https://eur-lex.europa.eu/legalcontent/EN/TXT/?qid=1599057203265&uri=CELEX:52020JC0008.

Farnell, T., Skledar Matijević, A. & Šćukanec Schmidt, N. (2021). *The Impact of COVID-19 on Higher Education: A Review of Emerging Evidence.* NESET Report. Publications Office of the European Union. https://doi.org/10.2766/069216216

Ferrario, M., Simm, W., Forshaw, S., Gradinar, A., Smith, M. & Smith, I. (2016). Values-First Software Engineering: Research Principles in Practice. In *Proceedings – International Conference on Software Engineering.* https://doi.org/10.1145/2889160.2889219

Findlay, A. M. (2011). An Assessment of Supply and Demand-Side Theorizations of International Student Mobility. *International Migration*, 49 (2), pp. 162–190.

Findlay, A., King, R., Stam, A. & Ruiz-Gelices, E. (2006). Ever Reluctant Europeans: The Changing Geographies of UK Students Studying and Working Abroad. *European Urban and Regional Studies*, 13 (4), pp. 291–318

Firebase Cloud Messaging (2021). Documentation. [Online, May 30, 2023]. https://firebase.google.com/docs/cloud-messaging

Flash Eurobarometer 466 (2018). *The European Education Area Report.* European Union: European Commission. https://ec.europa.eu/commfrontoffice/publicopinion/index.cfm/ResultDoc/download/DocumentKy/83257

Gacel-Ávila, J. (2005). The Internationalisation of Higher Education: A Paradigm for Global Citizenry. *Journal of Studies in International Education*, 9 (2), pp. 121–136.

Gao, Y., Baik, C. & Arkoudis S. (2015). *Internationalization of Higher Education.* In J. Huisman, H. de Boer, D. D. Dill & M. Souto-Otero (Eds.), *The Palgrave International Handbook of Higher Education Policy and Governance*. Palgrave Macmillan.

González, C. R., Mesanza, R. B. & Mariel, P. (2011). The Determinants of International Student Mobility Flows: An Empirical Study on the Erasmus Programme. *Higher education*, 62 (4), pp. 413–430.

Hermanowicz, J. C. (2018). *The Professoriate in International Perspective*. In M. B. Paulsen (Ed.), *Higher Education: Handbook of Theory and Research* (pp. 2399–293). Springer International Publishing.

Heryandi, A. (2018). Developing Application Programming Interface (API) for Student Academic Activity Monitoring Using Firebase Cloud Messaging (FCM). *IOP Conference Series: Materials Science and Engineering*, 012149. https://doi.org/10.1088/1757-899X/407/1/012149.

Heublein, U., Hutzsch, C. & Lörz, M. (2008). Auslandsmobilität deutscher Studierender: Ausmaß, Motive und Gründe des Desinteresses. *Bildung und Erziehung*, 61 (4), pp. 437–450.

Holloway, S. L., O'Hara, S. L. & Pimlott-Wilson, H. (2012). Educational Mobility and the Gendered Geography of Cultural Capital: The Case of International Student Flows between Central Asia and the UK. *Environment and Planning*, 44 (9), pp. 2278–2294.

Huang, F., Crăciun, D. & de Wit, H. (2022). Internationalization of Higher Education in a Post- Pandemic World: Challenges and Responses. *Higher Education Quarterly*, 76, pp. 203–212. https://doi.org/10.1111/hequ.12392.

Hunter, F., McAllister-Grande, B., Proctor, D. & de Wit, H. (2022). *The Evolving Definitions of Internationalization. A Question of Values.* In D. Deardorff, H. de Wit, B. Leask & H. Charles (Eds.), *Handbook on International Higher Education* (2nd ed., pp. 53–74). Stylus.

Ketunen, J. (2014). The Stakeholder Map in Higher Education. *International Proceedings of Economics Development and Research*, 78 (7), pp. 34–38.

King, R. & Ruiz-Gelices, E. (2003). International Student Migration and the European 'Year Abroad': Effects on European Identity and Subsequent Migration Behaviour. *International Journal of Population Geography*, 9 (3), pp. 229–252.

Knight, J. (2008). *Higher Education in Turmoil. The Changing World of Internationalization*. Sense Publishers.

Knight, J. & de Wit, H. (2018). Internationalization of Higher Education: Past and Future, *International Higher Education*, 95, pp. 2–4.

Maggio, Z. (2012). *Exploring Burton Clark's Triangle, A Symposium on Kerr's Life, Work and Legacy*. The Steinhardt Institute for Higher Education Policy, New York University.

Maringe, F. & Foskett, N. (2010). *Globalization and Internationalization in Higher Education. Theoretical, Strategic and Management Perspectives*. Continuum International.

Marshall, S. J. (2018). Internal and External Stakeholders in Higher Education. In *Shaping the University of the Future* (pp. 777–102). Springer Singapore.

Mittrick, M., Richardson, J., Asher, D., James, A. & Hanratty, T. (2018). *A Visualization Technique to Improve Situational Awareness.*

Murray, S., Ensign, W. & Yanagi, M. (2010). Combat Situation Awareness (CSA). *Model-Based Characterizations of Marine Corps Training and Operations,* 38.

Polak, M. (2018). Risk Management in Internationalisation of Higher Education. A Practical Institutional Approach. *Internationalisation of Higher Education,* 2. https://pw.academia.edu/MarekPolak

Pyvis, D. & Chapman, A. (2007). Why University Students Choose an International Education: A Case Study in Malaysia. *International Journal of Educational Development*, 27 (2), pp. 235–246.

Qazi, A., Qazi, J., Naseer, K., Zeeshan, M., Hardaker, G., Maitama, J. Z. & Haruna, K. (2020). Analyzing Situational Awareness through Public Opinion to Predict Adoption of Social Distancing Amid Pandemic COVID-19. *Human Factors and Ergonomics Society*, 92, pp. 849–855.

Qiang, Z. (2003). Internationalization of Higher Education: Towards a Conceptual Framework. *Policy Futures in Education*. 1 (2), pp. 248–270.

Robertson, S., Hoare, L. & Harwood, A. (2011). Returnees, Student-Migrants and Second Chance Learners: Case Studies of Positional and Transformative Outcomes of Australian International Education. *A Journal of Comparative and International Education*, 41 (5), pp. 685–698.

Rosenmund, M., Geiderer, D. & Kickingereder, S. (2012). Eine Studie zu Berichten österreichischer Erasmus-Studierender. Mit Erasmus durch Europa. *Österreichische Studierende Berichten üben ihren Auslandsaufenthalt,* pp. 25–115.

Roy, A., Newman, A., Ellenberger, T. & Pyman, A. (2019). Outcomes of International Student Mobility Programs: A Systematic Review and Agenda for Future Research. *Studies in Higher Education*, 44 (9), pp. 1630–1644.

Salazar, J. & Leihy, P. (2013). Keeping Up with Coordination: From Clark's Triangle to Microcosmographia. *Studies in Higher Education*, 38 (1) pp. 53–70.

Schmuller, J. (2001). *We Think in UML*. Grada.

Senge, P. M. (1990). *The Fifth Discipline: The Art and Practice of the Learning Organization*. Doubleday/Currency.

Smrčka, F., Musil, M. & Chalupová, M. (2022). Management System for Integration of the Disabled on the Labour Market. In *Proceeding of the 18th Conference on Management Leadership and Governance* (pp. 3822–988). ACPIL.

Strater, L., Endsley, M. R., Pleban, R. J. & Matthews, M. D. (2001). *Measures of Platoon Leader Situation Awareness in Virtual Decision-Making Exercises.*

Tosi, F., Impicciatore, R. & Rettaroli, R. (2019). 'Individual Skills and Student Mobility in Italy: a Regional Perspective'. *Regional Studies*, 53 (8), pp. 1099–1111.

Tran, L. T. (2016). Mobility as 'becoming': A Bourdieuian Analysis of the Factors Shaping International Student Mobility. *British Journal of Sociology of Education*, 37 (8), pp. 1268–1289.

Van Mol, C. (2013). Intra-European Student Mobility and European Identity: A Successful Marriage? *Population, Space and Place, Special Issue: International Student Migration*, 19 (2), pp. 209–222.

Van Mol, C. & Timmerman, C. (2014). Should I Stay or Should I Go? An Analysis of the Determinants of Intra-European Student Mobility. *Population, Space and Place*, 20 (5), pp. 465–479.

Voráček, J. & Přibyl, A. (2020). Cybersecurity Management: A Knowledge-Based Perspective. In *15th International Forum on Knowledge Asset Dynamics Proceedings* (pp. 219–234). Matera: University of Basilicata.

Voráček, J., Voráčková, W. & Schroeder, J. (2021). Situation Awareness and Governed Trust in Partner Networks: A Hierarchical Conceptual Model. In *16th International Forum on Knowledge Asset Dynamics Proceedings* (pp. 5455–565). Arts for Business Institute.

Wadhwa, R. (2018). International Student Mobility: Theoretical Context and Empirical Evidence From Literature. In *International Student Mobility and Opportunities for Growth in the Global Marketplace* (pp. 155–30). IGI Global.

Wang, C., Zhe Cheng, Z., Yue, X. G. & McAleer, M. (2020). Risk Management of COVID-19 by Universities in China. *Journal of Risk and Financial Management*, 13 (2).

Wihlborg, M. & Robson, S. (2018). Internationalisation of Higher Education: Drivers, Rationales, Priorities, Values and Impacts. *European Journal of Higher Education*, 8 (1), pp. 8–18.

Raja Suzana Raja Kasim and Nurul Azreen Salleh

4. Cultural and Philosophical Implications of Knowledge: Personalisation of Islamic Knowledge Management Practices in Developing Insaniah Value for Selected At-Risk Youth Groups in Malaysia – A Literature Review

Abstract: In Islamic perspectives, the believer's experience of the hereafter is determined by his actions. The Quran describes humankind as a fragile creature made of dust from the same earth they walk upon. The existence of the human being is like a coin that comes fashioned with two sides: a human is made in the best mould, fashioned with the breath of God's spirit, and on the other hand, a fragile creature. As fragile creatures, the knowledge dimensions of humans are challenged by their level of experience in anxiety, forgetfulness, ungratefulness, and vulnerability. As set in this chapter, the Islamic knowledge management practices address the management of knowledge of dimensions of human resides among fragile individuals that are selected at-risk youth groups. This chapter aims to model insaniah value as one of the core strategies to build good conduct while personalizing Islamic knowledge management practices in discovering, creating, and applying knowledge addressing the fragile nature of at-risk youth. The famous Persian scholar A. H. Al-Ghazali, regarding his Sufism approach, was analysed regarding the literature to offer and shed light on managing knowledge related to human spiritual levels, and faith-based dimensions, which are often overlooked. The insaniah value model will be an efficient and effective guide with knowledge of human beings that is managed in a more personalised manner. Therefore, the chapter offers cutting-edge research and a practical contribution to knowledge discovery, creation, and application in the contemporary developments of human capital.

Keywords: Knowledge Management Practices, youth at risk, Al-Ghazali, spirituality, Islamic, Malaysia

4.1. Introduction

Managing knowledge for the betterment and positive youth development in the modern Islamic perspectives appears to be underestimated. For example, managing knowledge discovery, creation, and application of knowledge related to mental health is in paramount need of innovative and subtlety approaches.

Mental health issues appear to be one of the many risky behaviours that young people are experiencing in Malaysia and also around the globe. According to World Health Organization in 2022, 50 % of mental health problems begin before age 14 and 75 % start in their 20s (Bernama, 2023). Statistics from the 2019 National Health and Morbidity Survey in Malaysia indicated that some 424,000 children are struggling with mental health problems. These are the potential youth groups who will become at risk in Malaysia. In this chapter, the youth is defined as being at risk when associated with one or multiple risk factors. Thus, the consequences among young people could be the physical and psychological problems associated with social issues. Youths are potentially at risk when their problems influence several people around them.

In Malaysia, social issues associated with youth at risk cut across a wide range of conditions that affect individuals. For example, gangsterism, juvenile delinquency, mental and physical disabilities, and drugs, alcohol, and other substance abuse adversely affect the community or people within a society, which may lead to mental health issues. From the Islamic perspective, building a good character means an alternative model for those who have experienced anxiety, forgetfulness, ungratefulness, and vulnerability, leading to mental health. In order to provide access to better personal well-being and productivity to vulnerable youths and at the same time safeguard the *maslahah* of the society, Al-Ghazali [1], through his model of Sufism, appears to offer a sound and innovative approach to counter social issues by understanding the core concept of knowledge and ways to manage this nature of knowledge. In this context, Al-Ghazali's concept of knowledge appears to be an essential part of this chapter. However, as there is an abundance of literature arguing about the true meaning of knowledge, this chapter will only cover personal knowledge management practices on the role of *'aql* which denotes intellect.

While in modern and contemporary science, knowledge management practices have been rooted in the work of Nonaka and Takeuchi (1995), Nonaka and Toyama (2003), Nonaka, Toyama, and Konno (1998), Nonaka, Toyama, and Nagata (2000), along with other scholars, Davenport and Prusak (1998); Polanyi (1966), Alavi and Leidner (2001), Kasim (2008), Zeleny (2006), to name few. The focus of interest in this chapter is on the work of Al-Ghazali's (2017) perspectives. Although Al-Ghazali (2017) and the modern perspectives such as Nonaka and Takeuchi (1995) are from two different schools of

1 Abū Hāmid Muhammad ibn Muhammad al-Ghazālī (1055–1111 AD) was one of the most famous Islamic scholars, thinkers and philosophers who lived in Persia. [Remark of the editor]

thought and science disciplines, both offer the same objectives in safeguarding knowledge management. In the light of assessing the ontological and Sufism perspective, the concept of data and knowledge will be revisited. This chapter also explores ways to personalize Islamic knowledge management practices that measure the knowledge of personal well-being and productivity among selected at-risk youths. A literature review was conducted on Al-Ghazali (2017) in his Sufism approach to offer and shed light on the spiritual and faith-based dimensions which are often overlooked. In addition, modelling *insaniah* (meaning: humanitarian) value is at the core of strategies to build good conduct, and spiritual and faith-based dimensions while personalizing Islamic knowledge management practices in discovering, creating, and applying knowledge.

Research integrating knowledge management practices (KMP), and the nature of knowledge as resides in the Sufism perspective, along with its influence to combat and manage knowledge discovery, creation, and application to tackle youth-at-risk issues and the extent to which personalised knowledge is managed, is still scant. Integrating modern personalised KMP and Islamic schools of thought also appeared to be infrequently researched. Though many have found some relationships between the KMP and various performances, be it at the individual and organisational levels (Sanchez, 2005, 1997; Adnan Jamaludin & Khairul Mizan, 2005). In this chapter, the objectives are briefly presented by the ideology of Al-Ghazali (2017) in the Sufism approach, and the chapter tries to evaluate if knowledge associated with youth-at-risk issues and problems can offer a new viewpoint addressing Sufism and personalised Islamic KMP.

4.2. Methodology

In this chapter, an extensive literature review was conducted to answer the chapter's objectives. Thus, a systematic review process is being expedited by database searches. As social issues are escalating among youth who in turn have the potential to become youth at-risk groups in Malaysia, a rapid approach to reviewing evidence was associated with the context of the COVID-19 pandemic. Several studies written in the Malay and English languages, published from 2014 onwards which included 15–25 years, were explored from the online ProQuest Dissertation database, engaging the manuscripts of Doctoral and Master's theses. This chapter aims to integrate multiple disciplines such as the broader perspective of positive youth development studies and management, behavioural science, knowledge management, and Sufism.

Hence, in gaining the meaning of successful management of knowledge and creating a model of *insaniah* value for selected at-risk groups, the role of personalization of Islamic KMP as one of the strategic resources in the 21st century will promote human values that are forward-looking with the provision of managing each aspect to discover, create, and apply knowledge. For this to happen, there is a need to revisit the role of personalised Islamic KMP in the contemporary perspectives using the Sufism approach by Al-Ghazali (2017).

A literature review investigated the keywords such as "Sufism", "Knowledge Management" and "at-risk youth" to capture empirical works from 2014 to 2022. The results projected 714 research works were conducted. However, despite the abundance of research accomplished associating these variables, the evaluation of Islamic KMP was limited. This was evidenced in the result yielding only four studies that associate "youth social issues" and "Al-Ghazali perspectives".

The association between the keywords of "knowledge conversion", "Nonaka & Takeuchi" and "youth issues" was investigated in further step. Publications were scoped and filtered among related applicable contexts such as the discovery in management, education, explicit knowledge, higher education, and competitive advantage. Only 42 past studies were found with different angles of approach and framework.

4.3. Literature Review

4.3.1. Al-Ghazali's Concept of Knowledge

Al-Ghazali's first definition of knowledge is related to the essence of cognition *(ma'rifah)*. Knowledge can also be defined as identifying an object known as it really is *('ala ma huwa bih)*. If the owner of the knowledge is able to act and deliver knowledge in an orderly fashion, knowledge is called a quality *(wasf)*. Knowledge from different perspectives appears to be treated as an image of an individual in the mirror of the intellect *('aql)*. According to Al-Ghazali's initial interpretation of knowledge it can be stated:

> There is no meaning to knowledge except that of its being an image ... that arrives in the soul, which conforms to that which is an image in sense perception, namely, the object known.
>
> Al-Ghazali (2017)

Despite many having argued that knowledge can be defined in multiple ways due to its nature of subtlety, and level of complexity, Al-Ghazali offers a different perspective. Asari (1993) concluded that Al-Ghazali's definition integrates division *(taqsïm)* and illustration *(mithal)*, as he wrote in the Ihya Ilmuddin, Fatihah, and, in a more general way in al-*Munqidh*.

The process of acquiring knowledge according to Sufism's way involves different activities. In one of Ghazali's popular books, *al-Munqidh*, managing knowledge appears to be intrinsically rooted in one's journey to get closer to God. This chapter is guiding readers to understand ways in managing personalised knowledge in accordance with the traditions of the Prophetic model, the Prophet of Islam (SAW), and in the light of the Quran, the revealed book of Islam.

As summarised in Table 4.1, Al-Ghazali's concept of knowledge offers three stages. The first stage relates to the inspirational optimistic message of Islam and flows in the understanding of knowledge on cleansing the heart from anything but God. Young people may have experience conflicts with family, the extreme stress of learning at schools, financial trouble, and unexpected illness which can manifest themselves in ways one may not anticipate. Building a strong connection with God can only be accomplished only after having the ability to exercise complete control over the qualities of the heart. Al-Ghazali pondered his perspective on knowledge which plays a key role in founding the social and moral edifice of Islam. Thus, the qualities of the heart lie in the way one is able to comprehend levels of heart purifications, adopt virtues and shun vices, observe good manners, and discharge obligations to others.

Next, the second stage, as indicated in Table 4.1, when young people are guided on ways to remembering God, then they will be taking away all forms of evil and forbidden acts. Thus, moral excellence, that state of quality of being good, righteousness, piety, humanness, generosity, kindness, honesty and integrity will be their characters. The good quality of characters denotes that the heart is being filled with the remembrance of God. As Asari (1993) claimed:

> This leads to a condition in which one experiences complete annihilation in God (*al-fana' bil-ku!liyah fi Allah*), when the heart becomes fully purified with a very high degree of preparedness and receptivity. When this condition is reached the spiritual realm becomes accessible, and one may see the angels, and the spirit of the prophets, and listen to and learn from them.
>
> Asari (1993)

Finally, as summarised in Table 4.1, Asari (1993) claimed that the merit of knowledge *(ilm)* is based on the heart's purity, preparedness, and receptivity, one might receive, through inspiration *(ilham)*, what al-Ghazali calls "the knowledge from on high *(al-'ilm al·laduni)*" or "the divine knowledge *(al-'ilm al·rabbëmÎ)*". Apart from the knowledge of the prophets that come through revelation *(wahyu)*, this is the highest knowledge one might have in this world. According to Quran, the man has many justifications for his actions but he knows what he is. This knowledge, 'he knows what he is', in fact human conscience, the Almighty God has given to everyone.

Human conscience is just like a lamp which is enkindled in every human mind and this nature of knowledge guides the man about what is right and what is wrong and what is good and what is evil. According to Chaudry (2006), one is treated as a good man, if the people say that he is good. The merit of knowledge or *ilm* is all about connectivity that God has given to everyone who is able to discover, create and apply the excellence of *'aql* as it rests upon the excellence of knowledge which is in itself excellent.

Table 4.1: Al-Ghazali's concept of knowledge

Stage	**Concept of Knowledge**
Stage 1	Cleansing the heart from anything but God
Stage 2	Filling the heart with remembrance of God
Stage 3	The merit of knowledge *(ilm)*

4.3.2. Personalised Islamic Knowledge Management Practices

There appears to be a great number of empirical studies associating the contemporary aspect of Knowledge Management Practices (KMP) on the performance of individuals and organisations. However, associating KMP in the perspectives of personalization and how it can deepen faith appears to be limited. The concept of success lies on the Islam's criterion to judge who is successful and its level of support towards excellence in knowledge. The contemporary perspectives treat a person successful when one is materially more wealthy, powerful and exercises a strong will and power. Spirituality aspects offer a unique way of throwing a person to balance in his connection with God. When the merit of knowledge offers excellence in one's life, the connection with God is getting stronger and spills over into an individual's belief system. The merit of knowledge leads to a success in thoughts and emotions, thus impacting spiritually and helps individuals in order to establish the worship of One God and spends in the way of God, perform all the practices, rituals and acts as prescribed by Islam.

The work of Awad and Sultan (2022) draw a picture of the man who is successful in the sight of Islam when he is able to rediscover the lens of growth and healing in managing the concept of success. Though Awad and Sultan (2022) focus on ways to manage knowledge among young people who experienced trauma and are emotionally distressed, the context appears to be relevant to position youth at risk to endure Islamic way of patterns, beliefs and ability to manage this nature of knowledge (Salleh, 1996; Asari, 1993).

Personalizing ways how to manage Islamic KMP offers a greater appreciation of life. In line with al-Ghazali in support of the excellence of knowledge, he concluded that the discussion of the problem is that knowledge is the basis of happiness *(al-sa'adah)* in the present world and in the world to come. Asari (1993) further claimed that happiness is the most excellent thing that can be attained by men, it follows that knowledge is also excellent. He arrives at this conclusion after going through a series of premises. He begins by stating that something precious and desired fall into either what is desired for its own inherent value, or what is desired as a means to achieve something else, or what is desired for both.

Ultimately, the greater spiritual development is all about the success that Allah gives to everyone who believes in Allah, in Prophets Muhammad (SAW) and in other prophets, in the Quran and Allah's other revealed books, and in the Day of Judgement and hereafter. Thus, happiness in the world to come is more desired than money because the former is sought for its own intrinsic value while the latter is sought as a means to gain something else Asari (1993). In the case of knowledge, Al-Ghazali says:

> know that knowledge is excellent in itself, without consideration of the thing known, so that even the knowledge of sorcery is excellent in itself, even though it be futile.
>
> Al-Ghazali (2017)

Asari (1993) argued that in addition to being excellent intrinsically, knowledge is also important for it to facilitate one to achieve the most valuable thing, that is, endless happiness *(al-sa'adah al-abadivah)*, and no one will attain this happiness without obeying the orders of God or without doing good deeds *('aman)*.

4.4. Conclusions

In conclusion, the link between the systematic way of managing Islamic KMP and faith-based doubts is important in many ways. Revisiting what has been prescribed by Islam and rewiring one's response to ways of managing Islamic knowledge can strengthen faith and have a profound effect on the positive development of every human being, including the spiritual part of ourselves.

However, as debated by scholars, no one can know what is good or evil without knowledge. The Islamic perspective on managing this nature of knowledge, such as obeying God and doing good deeds, requires the possession of knowledge. This means that eternal happiness can be achieved only through having knowledge. Al-Ghazali also points out that in the present world, knowledge presents its owner with honor, influence over those in power, and many other things which add to its merit. Accordingly, al-Ghazali puts knowledge as the basis of any other things and views, and it is the most excellent thing.

In managing and personalizing Islamic KMP, there are several classifications of knowledge. First, attaining eternal happiness means that knowledge is followed by good actions that lead one to that happiness. For example, the conduct of the Prophet Muhammad (SAW) is a model for a Muslim. The Quran calls his conduct very sublime and great. The title of *al-Sadiq* which means the truthful and *al-Ameen* (the trustworthy) exhibit excellent conduct and is a great factor in winning the hearts of the people to Islam.

Acknowledgments

The Ministry of Higher Education Malaysia Fundamental Research Grant Scheme supported this research.

The grant code is FRGS/1/2020/SS0/UMK/01/1.

References

Adnan Jamaludin & Khairul Mizan (2005). Knowledge Management and Competitive Advantage: A Conceptual Framework for Strategic Advantage. *Proceedings at the International Conference on Knowledge Management.* University Putra Malaysia, Putra World Trading Centre, Kuala Lumpur, Malaysia. 77–9 July 2005.

Al-Ghazāli, A. H. (2017). *Ihyā 'Ulūm al-Dīn. Jilid 1. Bab 2: pokok-pokok akidah* (Translated by: M. Akhyar, S. Jasah, pp. 279–381). Kuala Lumpur: Pustaka Al Shafa.

Alavi, M. & Leidner, D. E. (2001). Knowledge Management and Knowledge Management Systems: Conceptual Foundations and Research Issue. *MIS Quarterly*, 25 (1), pp. 1077–136.

Asari, H. (1993). *The Educational Thought of Al-Ghazali: Theory and Practice.* Unpublished Thesis, Masters of Arts. Montreal: Institute of Islamic Studies. McGill University.

Awad, N. & Sultan, S., (2022). *Your Lord Has Not Forsaken You: Addressing the Impact of Trauma on Faith.* United States of America: Yaqeen Institute for Islamic Research.

Bernama. (2023). *424,000 Children in Malaysia Grappling with Mental Health Problems.* https://www.freemalaysiatoday.com/category/nation/2022/04/18/424000-children-in-malaysia-grappling-with-mental-health-problems/

Chaudry, M. S. (2006). *Social and Moral Code of Islam.* Selangor. Malaysia: Masterpiece Publication Sdn. Bhd.

Davenport, T. H. & Prusak, L. (1998). *Working Knowledge: How Organizations Manage What They Know*. Boston: Harvard Business School Press.

Kasim, R. S. R. (2008). *Knowledge Management Practices in the Relationship between Corporate Strategies and Organizational Performances among Public-Listed Companies in Malaysia*. Unpublished Doctoral Dissertation. Serdang: Universiti Putra Malaysia.

Kasim, R. S. R. (2021). *The Contemporary Features of Islamic Business Model Theory: Understanding Spirituality*. University Malaysia Kelantan. https://youtu.be/ovEb6NyzDEs

Kasim, R. S. R. & Hashim, Z. (2018). *Pemerkasaan generasi muda komuniti terpinggir lulusan TVET dalam menangani cabaran arus Industri 4.0 ke arah Negara maju* (R. Raja Suzana & A. R. Samsudin, Ed.2.). Kota Bharu: Penerbit UMK.

Nonaka, I. & Takeuchi, H. (1995). *The Knowledge Company, How Japanese Companies Create the Dynamics of Innovation*. New York: Oxford University Press.

Nonaka, I. & Toyama, R. (2003). *The Knowledge-Creating Theory Revisited: Knowledge Creation as a Synthesizing Process*. http://www.proquest.umi.com

Nonaka, I., Toyama, R. & Konno. (1998). SECI, *Ba and Leadership: A Unified Model of Dynamic Knowledge-Creation*. http://www.proquest.umi.com

Nonaka, I., Toyama, R. & Nagata A. (2000). *A Firm as a Knowledge-Creating Entity: A New Perspective on the Theory of the Firm*. http://www.proquest.umi.com

Pollanyi, M. (1966). *The Tacit Dimension*. London: Routledge & Kegan Paul.

Salleh, K. (1996). An Examination on the Nature of al-Ghazali Sufism. *Islamiyyat*, 17, 47–63.

Sanchez, R. (1997). Managing Articulated Knowledge in Competence-Based Competition. In R. Sanchez & A. Heene (Eds.), *Strategic Learning and Knowledge Management* (pp. 161–187). Chichester: John Wiley & Sons.

Sanchez, R. (2005). *Knowledge Management and Organizational Learning: Fundamental Concepts for Theory and Practice*. http://www.lri.lu.se/pdf/wp/2004-3.pdf

Sohraby, B. & Abedin, B. (2005). A Web Designer Agenda, Based on Usage Mining Online Behavior of Visitor. In *Proceedings at the International Conference on Knowledge Management*. Kuala Lumpur, Malaysia: University Putra Malaysia, Putra World Trading Centre, 7–9 July 2005.

Daniela Hofmann

5. Wissen über Risiken als Entscheidungsgrundlage: Ehrenamtliche und ihre Motive unter besonderer Berücksichtigung ihrer Haftungsrisiken – eine empirische Untersuchung in Deutschland und Österreich

Zusammenfassung: In Deutschland wie auch in Österreich herrscht ein starker Wettbewerb um geeignete und motivierte Ehrenamtliche in Vorständen von Non-Profit-Organisationen (NPOs), respektive eingetragenen Vereinen. Mögliche zivilrechtliche Haftungsrisiken der ehrenamtlich Tätigen stehen in unmittelbarem Zusammenhang mit den jeweiligen Engagements, sind jedoch nicht immer hinreichend bekannt. Die Kenntnisse von den möglichen Haftungsrisiken variieren stark, doch im Grundsatz sind sie als eher gering einzustufen, selbst bei solchen Ehrenamtlichen, die bereits seit vielen Jahren in diversen Positionen ehrenamtlich tätig sind.

Neben den Kenntnissen von möglichen Haftungsrisiken variieren auch die Beweggründe zur Übernahme von Ehrenämtern stark. Die Konsequenzen, welche die Ehrenamtlichen aus der Kenntnis von möglichen Risiken ziehen, sind untrennbar mit den individuellen Motiven bzgl. des Ehrenamtes verbunden. Die Motivation des Einzelnen hängt kausal mit der individuellen Bereitschaft, ein Ehrenamt zu übernehmen bzw. ein bestehendes Ehrenamt fortzuführen, zusammen.

Als hilfreich hat sich die Einordnung in drei Typen von Ehrenamtlichen erwiesen: Typ A, der extrinsisch motiviert ist und sich dessen bewusst ist; Typ B, der ebenfalls extrinsisch motiviert ist, dem dies jedoch nicht bewusst ist und Typ C, der überwiegend intrinsisch motiviert ist. Mit der Festlegung überindividueller Gemeinsamkeiten sind Aspekte der Motivation und der Bereitschaft zur Übernahme von Haftungsrisiken gleichermaßen berücksichtigt. Dies erlaubt NPOs eine Zuordnung der (potenziellen) Ehrenamtlichen zu den herausgearbeiteten Typen und einen Rückschluss auf geeignete Maßnahmen bei der Rekrutierung und Bindung von Ehrenamtlichen. Diese Einordnung ist für alle am Rekrutierungsverfahren Beteiligten nachvollziehbar, wenn sie offen kommuniziert wird. Die Typenbildung kann von allen Arten an NPOs gleichermaßen eingesetzt werden, insbesondere auch von kleineren, in Personalmarketing unerfahrenen Organisationen. Die daraus resultierenden erforderlichen Maßnahmen kann sodann jede Organisation zugeschnitten auf ihre individuellen Bedürfnisse bestimmen.

Entscheidend ist, dass die Differenzierung der drei Ehrenamts-Typen in den kompletten Personalmarketingprozess eingebunden wird.

Letztlich bietet die Typenbildung sogar bestehenden oder potenziellen Ehrenamtlichen die Option, sich selbst und die eigenen Beweggründe kritisch zu hinterfragen.

Für den NPO-Sektor ergeben sich durch die Erkenntnisse aus der Typenbildung bessere Einsatzmöglichkeiten der Ressource Ehrenamtliche. Daraus ergibt sich ein ökonomischer Nutzen, der auch in NPOs ein nicht zu unterschätzender Aspekt ist. Die falsche Person im falschen Amt, daraus resultierende Nachteile und die erneute Suche nach einer geeigneteren Person können vermieden werden. Darüber hinaus können individuell abgestimmte Maßnahmen die intrinsische wie auch die extrinsische Motivation der Ehrenamtlichen erhöhen und zu einer verbesserten Organisationskultur führen. Eine Organisation mit einer guten Kultur ist wiederum attraktiver im Wettbewerb um geeignete und motivierte Ehrenamtliche.

Gute und motivierte Ehrenamtliche in den für sie geeigneten Ämtern führen in der Regel auch zu einer größeren Attraktivität der Organisation für ihre Mitglieder. Mitglieder, die vor der Entscheidung stehen, einer finanziell, strukturell und personell gut aufgestellten NPO beizutreten oder einer Organisation mit offensichtlichen Schwächen in diesen Bereichen, werden sich für erstere entscheiden. Von einer soliden Mitgliederzahl profitieren Organisation und Mitglieder gleichermaßen.

Schlagworte: Risiken, Ehrenamt, Haftung, Vereine, Non-Profit-Organisationen

5.1. Problemstellung

NPOs sehen sich einem zunehmend stärker werdenden Wettbewerb ausgesetzt (vgl. Bruhn, 2013, S. 5). Die Engagementquote bleibt mit 39,7 % stabil (Statista 2019a, S. 11), nimmt jedoch nicht in dem Maße zu wie der stärker werdende Wettbewerb es erfordern würde. Insbesondere in Leitungs- und Vorstandsfunktionen ist eine Abnahme der Bereitschaft festzustellen. Von 1999 bis 2019 sank der Anteil an Ehrenamtlichen in Führungspositionen von 36,8 % auf 26,3 % (vgl. Statista 2019a, S. 169). So geben beispielsweise 32 % der Sportvereine an, bei Akquise und Bindung von ehrenamtlichen Funktionsträgern/-innen ein „sehr großes Problem“ zu haben, welches die Existenz dieser Vereine bedroht. 23 % der Sportvereine bezeichnen die Gewinnung und Bindung der Funktionsträger/-innen als „großes Problem“ (Breuer & Feiler, 2019, S. 28).

Unabhängig von einer Zugehörigkeit zu einer der im Gesetz vorgesehenen Rechtsformen bestehen Haftungsrisiken grundsätzlich bereits mit kurzfristig geplanten Aktivitäten – wie etwa ein spontaner Spendenaufruf oder der Einsatz im Zuge von Hilfsmaßnahmen bei unvorhersehbaren Ereignissen durch Privatpersonen (vgl. Nowotny & Fida, 2007, S. 214). Finden die Aktivitäten im Rahmen einer rechtlich unstrukturierten Organisation statt, muss der Handelnde mit einer persönlichen Haftung im Außenverhältnis rechnen (vgl. Nowotny, 2013, S. 183) oder bei einer konkludent geschlossenen Gesellschaft alle an der Organisation (im Sinne einer Gesellschaft) beteiligten Personen (vgl. Nowotny, 2013, S. 184).

In Österreich gilt, dass „jedermann berechtigt ist, vom Schädiger Ersatz jenes Schadens zu verlangen, den ihm dieser rechtswidrig und schuldhaft zugefügt hat" (§ 1295 Allgemeines Bürgerliches Gesetzbuch, ABGB).

Der deutsche wie auch der österreichische Gesetzgeber haben die bestehenden Haftungsrisiken als unzumutbar für beispielsweise ehrenamtlich tätige Organe von Vereinen angesehen. Es kann gesagt werden, dass die jeweiligen Gesetzgeber die Haftung auf Schadensfälle, die durch grobe Fahrlässigkeit und Vorsatz beim Verein selbst verursacht wurden, beschränken wollen.

An diesem Punkt setzt die diesem Artikel zugrundeliegende Forschungsarbeit an. Sie widmet sich der grundsätzlichen Frage, welche Gründe die in Deutschland und Österreich unentgeltlich Mitarbeitenden in NPOs zu ihrem Engagement bewegen. Die Arbeit berücksichtigt hierbei insbesondere die trotz der Haftungsprivilegierungen noch immer vorliegenden Haftungsrisiken der unentgeltlich Tätigen, insbesondere jene in leitenden Funktionen.

Ziel der Untersuchung ist es, in einem internationalen Vergleich der Länder Österreich und Deutschland die unterschiedliche Begriffs- und Statusbestimmung von freiwillig Engagierten zu erörtern. Dem vorausgehend erfolgt kontextbezogen eine Einordnung und Definition des Begriffs NPO in den beiden Vergleichsländern Österreich und Deutschland. Darüber hinaus werden die Gründe für freiwilliges Engagement herausgearbeitet sowie bestehenden Haftungssituationen für Ehrenamtliche in den beiden Ländern aufgezeigt.

Ergänzend soll durch empirische Forschung in Erfahrung gebracht werden, inwiefern die noch immer bestehenden Haftungsrisiken eine Bereitschaft zum freiwilligen Engagement beeinflussen. Auch hier soll die Situation in den beiden Ländern gesondert betrachtet und dann miteinander verglichen werden.

Aus dieser Zielsetzung verbunden mit der oben dargestellten Problemstellung ergeben sich folgende Forschungsfragen, deren Analyse und Beantwortung den Kern der zugrundeliegenden Dissertation der Verfasserin bilden, die in diesem Artikel kurz umrissen wird.

Übergeordnete Gesamtforschungsfrage: Welche organisatorischen, wirtschaftlichen und rechtlichen Maßnahmen können einzelne NPOs zur Förderung der Bereitschaft zum Ehrenamt bzw. zur formellen Freiwilligenarbeit ergreifen?

Forschungsfrage 1: Welche Motive überwiegen bei der Übernahme von Ehrenamt/formeller Freiwilligenarbeit?

Forschungsfrage 2: Inwieweit kennen Ehrenamtliche/formelle Freiwillige ihre Haftungsrisiken?

Forschungsfrage 3: Welchen Einfluss haben bestehende Haftungsrisiken auf die Bereitschaft zum Ehrenamt/formellen Freiwilligenarbeit?

5.2. Non-Profit-Organisationen in Deutschland und Österreich

Im Rahmen des vorliegenden Berichtes wird von Non-Profit-Organisationen (NPOs) gesprochen, da dieser Begriff einprägsam ist und zum anderen international, insbesondere im angelsächsischen Bereich, stärker vertreten ist (vgl. Zimmer, 2001, S. 7).

Innerhalb der NPOs sind drei Idealtypen der Organisationen zu unterscheiden. Zum einen gibt es die sogenannte *Spenderorganisation*, welche sich durch Spenden finanziert. Diese Organisationsform bietet unentgeltliche vermögenswerte Leistungen an wie beispielsweise karitative Organisationen, deren Ziel etwa die Minimierung von Elend in der Dritten Welt ist (vgl. v. Hippel, 2005, S. 89). *Mitgliedernützige Organisationen* hingegen finanzieren sich mittels Zahlungen ihrer Mitglieder. Im Gegenzug erhalten die Mitglieder vermögenswerte Leistungen (vgl. v. Hippel, 2005, S. 89). *Kommerzielle NPOs* finanzieren sich durch Zahlungen außenstehender Personen, die im Gegenzug zur Zahlung vermögenswerte Leistungen erhalten. Hierzu gehören beispielsweise Kindergärten, Krankenhäuser etc. (vgl. v. Hippel, 2005a, S. 90).

Der deutsche Nonprofit-Sektor wird maßgeblich durch das sogenannte Subsidiaritätsprinzip bestimmt. Das Subsidiaritätsprinzip ist ein „Prinzip, das auf die Entfaltung der individuellen Fähigkeiten, der Selbstbestimmung und Selbstverantwortung abstellt. Nur dort, wo die Möglichkeiten des Einzelnen bzw. einer kleinen Gruppe nicht ausreichen, Aufgaben zu lösen, sollen staatliche Institutionen subsidiär eingreifen. Dabei ist der Hilfe zur Selbsthilfe der Vorrang vor einer unmittelbaren Aufgabenübernahme durch den Staat zu geben“ (Suchanek, 2021). Das Subsidiaritätsprinzip gewährt den NPOs bei der Erbringung von Wohlfahrtsleistungen einen Vorzug gegenüber staatlichen Interventionen (vgl. Winheller, 2010, S. 44). Ausdruck des Subsidiaritätsprinzips sind zum einen mit dem Staat eng verbundene und von diesem subventionierte Wohlfahrtsverbände, die jedoch trotzdem selbständig sind. Zum anderen gehen aus dem Subsidiaritätsprinzip auch solche Organisationen hervor, die im Bereich der Freizeit, der Kultur, des Sports und der Umwelt mit ihrer Einrichtung der Forderung nach bürgerschaftlichem Engagement vor dem staatlichen Handeln folgen und sich insbesondere durch ehrenamtliche Mitarbeit und eine Eigenfinanzierung durch Spenden auszeichnen (vgl. Zimmer & Priller, 2007, S. 14, 24). NPOs in Deutschland sind darüber hinaus durch die Grundsätze der Selbstverwaltung und der Gemeinwirtschaft geprägt (vgl. Winheller, 2010, S. 45). Das Prinzip der Gemeinwirtschaft beruht auf dem Hauptziel der Verbesserung von sozialen und ökonomischen

Rahmenbedingungen und nicht der Gewinnmaximierung wie bei kapitalwirtschaftlichen Unternehmungen (vgl. Anheier & Seibel, 2004, S. 10–11, 18–19, 72–73).

Grundsätzlich stehen als Organisationsformen für NPOs alle gesetzlich normierten Rechtsformen, wie beispielsweise Vereine, Stiftungen, aber auch GmbH etc. zur Verfügung, wobei in der Anzahl der deutschen NPOs die Vereine mit 51,7 % überwiegen (vgl. Statista, 2019a, S. 166).

Die Tatsache, dass Österreich ein Bundesstaat mit neun Bundesländern ist, die jedes ein autonomes Landesgesetz haben (vgl. Republik Österreich, 2019), wirkt sich grundlegend auf die NPO-Struktur in Österreich aus. Eine große Anzahl von NPOs ist auf Landesebene organisiert und wendet dort die spezifischen Länder-Sozialgesetze und Finanzierungsmodelle an. Das führt dazu, dass mitunter Schwesterorganisationen in verschiedenen Bundesländern eine gänzlich andere Ausprägung haben (vgl. Pennerstorfer et al., 2013, S. 55). Nur wenige NPOs sind auf Bundesebene organisiert (ebenda).

Wesentlich im österreichischen NPO-Sektor ist außerdem der Umstand, dass es zahlreiche berufsständische Interessenvertretungen gibt, deren Mitgliedschaft zum Teil freiwillig ist, jedoch auch gesetzlich verpflichtend sein kann (ebenda). Vorliegend werden nur diejenigen Interessenvertretungen als NPOs betrachtet, deren Mitgliedschaft freiwillig ist. Die berufsständischen Interessenvertretungen sind insofern bedeutsam, als sie oftmals einen großen politischen Einfluss haben, der in dieser Form im internationalen Vergleich eher ungewöhnlich ist (vgl. Pennerstorfer et al., 2013, S. 56).

In Österreich sind NPOs in der Regel als Genossenschaften, Vereine oder Stiftungen organisiert. Andere Rechtsformen (z.B. GmbH und AG) sind jedoch ebenfalls möglich.

Die Gemeinnützigkeit ist in Österreich genauso wenig wie in Deutschland mit Non-Profit-Organisationen gleichzusetzen. Ebenso wie in Deutschland wird die Gemeinnützigkeit von den Finanzbehörden geprüft.

5.3. Ökonomische Grundlagen

Bedeutende gesellschaftlich erforderliche Leistungen werden wie bereits dargestellt u. a. von NPOs erbracht. So werden die NPOs zu einem unabkömmlichen Teil des sozialen und kulturellen Lebens, der Gesellschaft insgesamt (vgl. Mayerhofer & v. Eckardstein, 2001, S. 226). Gleichzeitig sehen sie sich jedoch der großen Problematik der (Selbst-) Finanzierung ausgesetzt.

In Deutschland bestehen 64,3 % der Einnahmen in Mitteln der öffentlichen Hand (z. B. Leistungsentgelte der Sozialversicherungen), international liegt hier der Anteil bei nur 42 %, in Österreich bei 50 % (vgl. Meyerhofer & v. Eckardstein, 2001, S. 225).

In NPOs stellt sich die Mitarbeiterstruktur oftmals dergestalt dar, dass es eine ehrenamtliche Leitungsebene gibt, welche strategische Verantwortung innehat. Die Mitglieder dieser Leitungsebene werden je nach Rechtsform Präsident oder Vorstand genannt (vgl. Helmig & Boenigk, 2019, S. 99). Je nach Rechtsform kann es zusätzlich zu den ehrenamtlichen Führungskräften hauptamtliche Führungskräfte geben (beispielsweise den Geschäftsführer der deutschen gGmbH oder hauptamtlichen Vorstand einer deutschen gAG). Diese hauptamtlichen Führungskräfte vertreten die Organisation dann ebenfalls nach außen.

Auf der ausführenden, der operativen Ebene sind je nach NPO allein Ehrenamtliche tätig oder teilen sich die anfallenden Aufgaben mit hauptamtlichen Mitarbeitern. Wesentlicher Unterschied zwischen den hauptamtlichen Mitarbeitern und den Ehrenamtlichen ist die Tatsache, dass die Hauptamtlichen aufgrund Arbeitsvertrages Arbeitnehmer sind, während die Ehrenamtlichen mit ihrem Engagement eine Zeitspende erteilen und eben keine Angestellten sind.

Zusammenfassend sind folgende Kriterien charakteristisch für ein Ehrenamt:

- die freiwillige Übernahme einer Ehrenamtsfunktion
- die gemeinschaftsbezogene Ausübung
- die Ausübung im öffentlichen Raum
- die Ausübung ohne Gewinnerzielungsabsicht
- die Orientierung am Gemeinwohl
(vgl. Statista 2019a, S. 18–20)

Es ist festzuhalten, dass das Personal in NPOs den bedeutendsten (Erfolgs-) Faktor zur Erfüllung der jeweiligen Mission darstellt, weshalb auch das Personalmanagement in NPOs eine große Bedeutung hat (vgl. Helmig & Boenigk, 2019, S. 99). Idealerweise erfolgt dies durch ein NPO-spezifisches Management des Personals, welches oft vielschichtig ist und unterschätzt wird (vgl. Simsa, 2003, S. 71).

Als Definition für Personalmanagement in NPOs wird u. a. vorgeschlagen, es als Aufgabe zu sehen, „das Personal einer Nonprofit-Organisation auf einem erwünschten Qualitätsniveau zu angemessenen Kosten zu gewinnen, zu erhalten, zu entwickeln und dieses wirtschaftlich in den Leistungsprozessen der Nonprofit-Organisation einzusetzen“ (Helmig & Boenigk, 2019, S. 99).

5.4. Motivation von Ehrenamtlichen

Motivation ist zu definieren als emotionale Erfahrung mit einer bestimmten Zielrichtung. Sie setzt ein aktuelles Motiv oder Bedürfnis voraus, dessen

Befriedigung von der betroffenen Person als realistisch angesehen wird (vgl. Breyter, 2022).

Wenn freiwillig Mitarbeitende weitgehend unentgeltlich tätig werden, muss es zusätzlich andere Motivationsgründe (intrinsische Motivation) geben als monetäre, extrinsische Motivatoren (vgl. Frey & Jegen, 2001, S. 589) bzw. geldwerten Anreize. Dem Gedanken, dass sich Mitarbeiter von materiellen Anreizen leiten lassen, folgt die sog. Agency-Theory bzw. Agenturtheorie (vgl. Ebers & Gotsch, 2014, S. 213–214). Der sog. *Stewardship-Ansatz* (Davis et al., 1997, S. 21) geht von einem Menschenbild aus, nach dem Menschen auch Aspekte wie

- Verantwortung übernehmen,
- „Leistung als Eigenwert",
- eigenverantwortliche Übernahme von Tätigkeiten zur Erreichung der Unternehmensziele,
- Selbstverwirklichung etc.

als motivierend ansehen (vgl. Mroß, 2009, S. 180).

In der Literatur werden zahlreiche Motivationstheorien vorgestellt, beispielsweise die wissenschaftliche Betriebsführung (vgl. Taylor, 1913, S. XII, S. 22), das Freiburger Management-Modell (Lichtsteiner et al., 2020), die Theorie der zwei Faktoren (Herzberg et al., 2010), die Gleichheits- oder Equity-Theorie (vgl. Adams, 1963, S. 427–430; s. weitergehend Kreitner & Kinicki, 2013, S. 213 ff.), die Anreiz-Beitragstheorie (vgl. Simon, 1991, S. 34) etc.

Motivation kann intrinsisch sein (wenn die Tätigkeit um ihrer selbst willen erfolgt, z. B., weil sie Spaß macht, weil sie sinnhaft ist, weil eigene Interessen befriedigt werden oder sie herausfordernd ist). Sie kann auch extrinsisch sein, wenn die Leistung mit dem Ziel erbracht wird, einen Vorteil zu erlangen oder einen Nachteil zu vermeiden (vgl. Helmig & Boenigk, 2019, S. 111).

5.5. Rechtliche Grundlagen

Bis ins Jahr 2009 war die Haftungssituation für im Verein ehrenamtlich Tätige schwierig. (Für die weitere Darstellung wird der Begriff des Ehrenamtlichen als Funktionsträger im Sinne eines Organs zugrunde gelegt.) Nach Einschätzung des Gesetzgebers waren die drohenden Haftungsrisiken geeignet, interessierte Ehrenamtliche davon abzuhalten, ein Ehrenamt in einem Verein zu übernehmen (vgl. zur rechtspolitischen Beurteilung: Leuschner, 2014, S. 283 ff.). Der am 03.10.2009 (BGBl. 09 I 3161) in Kraft getretene und durch Gesetz vom 21.03.2013 (Ehrenamtsstärkungsgesetz vom 21.03.2013 in BGBl, I S. 556) geänderte § 31a BGB soll durch Haftungsbeschränkungen des Vorstandes oder der besonderen Vertreter gegenüber dem Verein und dessen Mitgliedern

(Innenverhältnis), § 31a I BGB, sowie das Einräumen eines Befreiungsanspruchs gegenüber dem Verein bei Haftung im Außenverhältnis, § 31a II S. 1 BGB (vgl. Dröner, 2019, § 31 a BGB, Rn. 1), die Bereitschaft zum Ehrenamt als Mitglied eines Vereinsorgans fördern (vgl. Leuschner, 2018, § 31a BGB, Rn. 1). Zur Beschränkung der Haftungsrisiken auf einen zumutbaren Umfang enthält der § 31a BGB eine Befreiung der ehrenamtlich tätigen Organmitglieder für einfach fahrlässig verursachte Schäden (ebenda).

Das am 01.07.2002 in Kraft getretene Bundesgesetz über Vereine (Vereinsgesetz, 2002 – VerG) stellt ebenfalls eine Reform des Vereinswesens in Österreich dar. Es löst das bis dahin geltende Vereinsrecht aus dem Jahr 1951 (BGBl Nr. 233/1951) ab. Durch das neuen Vereinsgesetz sollen Haftungsrisiken verringert und damit das Ehrenamt gestärkt werden (vgl. Bundesministerium für Justiz Österreich, 2017, Enquete zum Vereinsrecht, S. 1).

In Deutschland gibt es auf Bundesländer-Ebene einen Haftpflichtversicherungsschutz für ehrenamtlich Tätige in Sammelverträgen, die alle Länder abgeschlossen haben, um einen Minimalschutz für die Fälle zu bieten, in denen eine andere Absicherung (beispielsweise eine private Haftplicht, die auch ehrenamtliches Engagement abdeckt) nicht besteht (exemplarisch Land Nordrhein-Westfalen, 2020).

5.6. Empirische Untersuchung zur Bereitschaft im Ehrenamt

Um die notwendigen Informationen zur Bearbeitung der Forschungsfragen zu erheben, wurden im Rahmen der zugrundeliegenden Dissertation halbstrukturierte, durch einen Leitfaden gestützte Interviews durch die Verfasserin genutzt. Diese Interviewform stellt einen Kompromiss zwischen dem reinen Erzählenlassen und dem Festhalten an vorgegebenen Fragen dar (vgl. Bock, 1992, S. 94). Der Verfasserin war es wichtig ist, die Interviewpartner zwar reden zu lassen, aber sicherzustellen, dass auch alle bedeutsamen Fragen gestellt werden. Insbesondere da die Verfasserin davon ausgeht, dass Unklarheiten im Rechtsteil der Fragen aufkommen können bzw. nähere Erläuterungen mit Beispielen notwendig werden können, war nach Auffassung der Verfasserin diese Interviewform hier am besten geeignet.

Der Leitfaden wurde in sieben Abschnitte unterteilt:

Abschnitt 1	• Biografische Eckdaten • Allgemeine Fragen zur ehrenamtlichen Tätigkeit • Art des Vereins • Dauer des Ehrenamts

Abschnitt 2	• Gründe für Mitgliedschaft • Gründe für Ehrenamt
Abschnitt 3	• Verständnis von Ehrenamt • Einbettung in Familien- bzw. soziales Leben
Abschnitt 4	• Detailfragen zur Tätigkeit im Vorstand
Abschnitt 5	• Einschätzung zur Vorbereitung auf das Ehrenamt
Abschnitt 6	• Kenntnisse nach zivilrechtlichen Rahmenbedingungen
Abschnitt 7	• Einfluss von Haftungsrisiken auf die Bereitschaft zum Ehrenamt

Zur Überprüfung der Klarheit und Praktikabilität wurde der Leitfaden einem Pretest unterzogen. Danach wurden die sechs Interviewpartner ausgewählt, die die notwendigen Merkmale

- ehrenamtliche/formell freiwillige Tätigkeit in einer NPO,
- Funktion als Mitglied eines Organs,
- Organ eines Vereins

erfüllten. Alle genannten Kriterien mussten kumulativ vorliegen. Somit ergab sich die folgende Teilnehmerliste für die Tiefeninterviews.

Tabelle 5.1: Probanden der Tiefeninterviews

Beruf	Sitz des Vereins	Alter	Geschlecht	Dauer der ehrenamtlichen Tätigkeit	Funktion im Ehrenamt
Rentner	Deutschland	75	m	10 Jahre	Vorstandsvorsitzender Tennisverein
Medizinische Fachangestellter	Deutschland	54	w	3 Jahre	Kassenwart Reitsportverein
Hochschuldozent	Deutschland	48	m	immer wieder seit ca. 30 Jahren	diverse Funktionen in z. T. führenden Positionen
Hochschulprofessor	Österreich Niederlande	32	m	seit ca. 15 Jahren	diverse Funktionen in z. T. führenden Positionen
Hochschulprofessor	Österreich Deutschland	52	m	immer wieder seit ca. 30 Jahren	diverse Funktionen in z. T. führenden Positionen
Zahnarzt	Deutschland	41	w	immer wieder seit ca. 10 Jahren	diverse Funktionen in z. T. führenden Positionen

Quelle: eigene Darstellung

5.6.1. Auswertung der Daten

Ziel der Auswertung im Rahmen dieser Forschung war es, mittels der Tiefeninterviews herauszufinden, welche Gemeinsamkeiten hinsichtlich der Motivation von Ehrenamtlichen vorliegen und diese von den individuellen Konstrukten der befragten Personen zu trennen, um sie, wenn möglich, zu einer Theorie zusammenzuführen. Für Forschungen, die als Ziel die Identifikation des „überindividuell Gemeinsamen" (Lang et al., 2020, S. 19) der Interviewpartner hat, bietet sich die qualitative Inhaltsanalyse in Form der Zusammenfassung an (ebenda). Die Möglichkeit der Wahl zwischen induktiver und deduktiver Kategorienbildung als Technik der Zusammenfassung bei Mayring (vgl. Mayring, 2020, S. 17) bot in dieser Forschung Vorteile. Zwar ergaben sich auf der Grundlage der theoretischen Forschung Hauptkategorien, die auch bereits in die Gliederung des Interviewleitfadens eingeflossen sind, jedoch war eine abschließende Kategorienbildung ex ante nicht möglich, da das Thema noch weitgehend unerforscht ist und sich im Rahmen der Interviews weitere Aspekte ergeben haben, die in der Form nicht zu erwarten waren. Es war also für die Beantwortung der vorliegenden Forschungsfragen bedeutsam, bei der Auswertung für die Bildung weiterer Kategorien offen zu bleiben.

Zudem war nach Auffassung der Verfasserin von Bedeutung, in welcher Häufigkeit bestimmte Gründe für das Ehrenamt, auch in Relation zum individuellen Kenntnisstand der Interviewten von den Haftungsrisiken, genannt werden. Dies stellte eine quantitative Ausrichtung der Auswertung dar. Mithin war für die vorliegende Forschung die Kombination der Auswertungsmethoden der qualitativen Inhaltsanalyse nach Mayring in Kombination mit der selbständigen Codierung besonders geeignet.

Für die Auswertung im Rahmen einer qualitativen Inhaltsanalyse stehen diverse Computerprogramme zur Verfügung. Für eine Anwendung des Programms QCAmap (Mayring, 2020) entschied sich die Verfasserin aufgrund der interaktiven Möglichkeiten dieser Webapplikation und der jederzeitigen Nachvollziehbarkeit des Analyseprozesses. Insbesondere die Regelgeleitetheit und die Überprüfbarkeit waren, wie bereits dargestellt, besonders wichtig, da die Autorin nicht in einer Forschungsgruppe arbeitet und demnach auch hinsichtlich Reliabilität der Auswertung auf ein System angewiesen war, welches zum einen in sich schlüssig ist und welches weiterhin das Ablaufmodell einer qualitativen Inhaltsanalyse in einem abgeschlossenen System vereint. Zudem ist überzeugend, dass die Kategorien auf der Grundlage eines vordefinierten Abstraktionsniveaus formuliert werden (ebenda). Eine weitergehende Einordnung in Hauptkategorien, denen die induktiv gebildeten Kategorien in Gruppen zugeordnet werden, ist ein weiterer hilfreicher Aspekt im Rahmen der Auswertung mit QCAmap (vgl. Mayring, 2020, S. 12), da hierdurch Gemeinsamkeiten bei den Kategorien schnell erkennbar werden.

5.6.2. Diskussion der Ergebnisse

5.6.2.1. Ergebnisse der Kategorienbildung

Ergebnisse zu Forschungsfrage 1

Bzgl. Forschungsfrage 1 führte die induktive Kategorienbildung für alle sechs Interviews zur Bildung der folgenden Hauptkategorien (dunkel) und Subkategorien.

Tabelle 5.2: Kategorien zu Forschungsfrage 1

Gründe für Ehrenamt im Verein
Gründe für Ehrenamt im Verein
Motivation Mitglied zu werden
Positive Erfahrungen im Ehrenamt
Gründe gegen Ehrenamt im Verein
Gründe gegen Ehrenamt im Verein
Schwierigkeiten im Ehrenamt
Negative Erfahrungen im Ehrenamt
Verständnis von Ehrenamt
Verständnis von Ehrenamt
Vorbereitung auf Ehrenamt
Zusammenarbeit im Vorstand
Anzahl Mitglieder
Aufeinandertreffen Haupt- und Ehrenamtliche
Unentgeltlichkeit

Quelle: eigene Darstellung

Hauptkategorie „Gründe für Ehrenamt im Verein"

Die von den Probanden angeführten Gründe, warum sie das oder die Ehrenämter übernommen haben, variierten stark.

Zusammenfassend ergaben sich die Motive der Interviewten zum Ehrenamt primär aus der Intention „zu helfen/Gutes zu tun". Dieses Motiv gaben alle sechs Probanden an, wobei das Helfen als Oberbegriff zu sehen ist und auch die Begünstigten sich unterscheiden. Allen Probanden der vorliegenden Forschung war es zudem wichtig, dass die Tätigkeit „sinnhaft" ist.

Zudem war allen der Erfolg in ihrer Tätigkeit wichtig. Hierbei unterschieden die Probanden selbst zwischen einem erfolgreichen Managen des Vereins in Form von Mitgliedergewinnung/Unterstützung der Mitglieder und Herstellung eines finanziell soliden Vereins, über die erfolgreiche Durchführung von Kampagnen bis hin zu positivem Feedback für geleistete Arbeit.

Positives Feedback von Vereinsmitgliedern oder Externen war allen Probanden wichtig und für alle ein wesentlicher Beweggrund, das Ehrenamt fortzuführen. Auffällig war, dass bei zwei von sechs Interviewten ein starker inhaltlicher Bezug zwischen der ehrenamtlichen Tätigkeit und dem Beruf der Probanden bestand.

Ein Unterschied zwischen den Motiven der Ehrenamtlichen in Deutschland und Österreich konnte in der vorliegenden Untersuchung nicht festgestellt werden.

Die dargestellten Ergebnisse entsprechen den Erkenntnissen aus der Theorie. Wenn unter dem Beweggrund „dem Gemeinwohl dienen wollen" zumindest „Gutes tun" und „helfen wollen" zu verstehen ist, so stimmten diesem Motiv bei einer 2019 durchgeführten Umfrage in Deutschland 89,1 % der ehrenamtlich tätigen Frauen und 85,9 % der ehrenamtlich tätigen Männer zu (Statista, 2019a). In einer ähnlich angelegten Befragung gaben in Österreich 58 % der Befragten an, mit ihrem Ehrenamt helfen zu wollen (Statista 2012/2013, Daten nach BMASGK, Österreich).

Hauptkategorie „Gründe gegen Ehrenamt im Verein"

Im Zusammenhang mit den Gründen gegen ein Ehrenamt ist festzuhalten, dass zeitliche und gesundheitliche Gründe im Vordergrund standen.

Zwei Probanden sahen das Ehrenamt auch pragmatisch und erkannten, dass es Situationen geben kann, in denen es zugunsten des Vereins einen Führungswechsel geben sollte.

Lediglich für einen Probanden sprachen die bestehenden Haftungsrisiken gegen ein Ehrenamt.

Mangelnde Akzeptanz von Meinungen und Entscheidungen hatten bei einem Teil der Probanden zwar schon zu Zweifeln am Ehrenamt geführt, letztlich aber keinen Grund dargestellt, das jeweilige Amt niederzulegen.

Die Ergebnisse der vorliegenden Forschung führten zu der Schlussfolgerung, dass für das Niederlegen der Ämter überwiegend solche Gründe genannt wurden, die außerhalb der Tätigkeit selbst liegen. Gesundheit und Zeit sind auch nicht von den Vereinen beeinflussbar. Der Faktor Spaß und auch die inhaltlichen Themen hingegen sind Aspekte, die von den Vereinen zumindest zu einem Teil beeinflusst werden können. Die Haftungsrisiken als Rahmenbedingung können ebenfalls von den Vereinen durch geeignete Maßnahmen minimiert bzw. sogar ganz ausgeschlossen werden.

Eine österreichische Studie zur Freiwilligenarbeit (IFES, 2016, S. 78) beleuchtet u. a. die Gründe, warum keine Ehrenämter übernommen werden und kommt zu dem Ergebnis, dass von den Befragten als wichtigster Grund genannt wird, sie seien nicht gefragt/gebeten worden. Ein Vergleich mit diesem Aspekt war an dieser Stelle nicht möglich, da alle Probanden der hier gegebenen Studie im Amt sind/waren und in den weit überwiegenden Fällen auch gebeten wurden, diese Ämter zu übernehmen. Auch der Aspekt, nicht darüber nachgedacht zu haben, war hier nicht vergleichbar, da alle Probanden Ämter innehaben/innehatten. Lediglich der dritte Aspekt des Ausgefülltseins durch familiäre Aufgaben konnte hier aufgegriffen werden. Alle sechs Probanden hatten zum Zeitpunkt der Interviews Familie und trotzdem ein oder mehrere Ämter inne. Dennoch gaben fünf der sechs Probanden an, dass sie aus familiären Gründen kein weiteres Amt übernehmen möchten. Daher deckt sich das Ergebnis der vorliegenden Studie diesbezüglich mit der österreichischen Studie. Mangels deutscher Studien zu Gegengründen im Ehrenamt konnte ein Vergleich mit anderen Studien an dieser Stelle nicht erfolgen.

In den vorliegenden Interviews wurden an insgesamt 192 Stellen Gründe *für* ein Ehrenamt aufgeführt. Demgegenüber stehen an 55 Stellen Gründe *gegen* ein Ehrenamt. Dies spricht dafür, dass die Befragten überwiegend positiv über das jeweilige Ehrenamt denken.

Hauptkategorie „Verständnis von Ehrenamt"

Hinsichtlich der individuellen Vorstellung von Ehrenamt ist anzumerken, dass bei allen Interviewten der Faktor des kostenlosen Zurverfügungstellens der eigenen Leistung, Wissen und Zeit als wesentliches Merkmal für Ehrenamt genannt wurde, wobei der Aspekt der Nicht-Bezahlung stets der zuerst genannte Aspekt war. Keiner der Probanden nahm zum Zeitpunkt der Interviews die gesetzlich vorgesehene Möglichkeit der Ehrenamtspauschale in Anspruch. Unabhängig von den oben bereits genannten Gründen für ein Ehrenamt hatten alle Probanden die Vorstellung vom Ehrenamt, ein zufriedenstellendes Engagement zu betreiben.

Hinsichtlich der Vorbereitung auf die Ehrenämter ist festzustellen, dass zwei Probanden nicht speziell auf ihre Tätigkeiten vorbereitet waren, jedoch keine Unsicherheit verspürten, da sie die Tätigkeit anderer Vorstandsmitglieder eine Zeit lang beobachtet hatten, bevor sie selbst Vorstandsposten übernahmen.

Auffällig ist, dass 50 % der Befragten angaben, mit ihrem Vorstand einen kompletten Vorstand abgelöst und dabei jeweils große Schwierigkeiten bei der Übergabe durch den alten Vorstand gehabt zu haben.

Ergebnisse zu Forschungsfrage 2

Bezüglich der Forschungsfrage 2 führte die induktive Kategorienbildung zur Bildung der folgenden Hauptkategorien und Subkategorien.

Tabelle 5.3: Kategorien zu Forschungsfrage 2

Keine Kenntnis vom Haftungsrisiko
Keine Kenntnis vom Haftungsrisiko
Kenntnis von D&O Versicherung
Kenntnis D&O Versicherung
Kenntnisnahme während des Amtes
Kenntnisnahme während des Amtes
Gute Kenntnis vom Haftungsrisiko
Erfahrungen mit Risiken
Grundkenntnisse vom Haftungsrisiko

Quelle: eigene Darstellung

Hauptkategorie „Keine Kenntnis vom Haftungsrisiko"

Drei Probanden waren hinsichtlich möglicher zivilrechtlicher Haftungsprobleme ohne jede Kenntnis und erfuhren erst im Interview von Risiken. Bemerkenswert ist, dass ein Proband keinerlei Kenntnisse hatte, obwohl er bereits seit 15 Jahren in diversen Vereinen aktiv gewesen war und auch seit einigen Jahren einen Vorstandsposten bzw. den Posten des Vorstandsvorsitzenden innehatte.

Die Dauer des ehrenamtlichen Engagements hat also offensichtlich keine Auswirkungen auf die Kenntnis der Risiken. Auch der Bildungsgrad hat keine Auswirkungen auf die Kenntnisse oder ein verstärktes Problembewusstsein. Inhaltlich und rechtlich war keiner der Probanden auf die Tätigkeit als Mitglied des Vorstandes geschult worden. Die Aufklärung bzgl. möglicher Haftungsrisiken ist offensichtlich nicht Bestandteil der Amtseinführung von Ehrenamtlichen in Vereinen.

Hauptkategorie „Kenntnis von D&O Versicherung"

Keiner der sechs Probanden kannte namentlich eine D&O Versicherung. Selbst der Proband, der von einem befreundeten Anwalt über die möglichen Haftungsrisiken eines Ehrenamtlichen informiert worden war, kannte die Möglichkeit einer Versicherung gegen Vermögensschäden, die anlässlich eines Ehrenamtes verursacht werden, nicht. Auch der Proband, der bereits negative Erfahrungen in seinen Ehrenämtern gemacht hatte, kannte die Möglichkeit einer Versicherung nicht. Ein Proband wusste zwar, dass sein Verein eine Versicherung abgeschlossen hat, mit der ein mögliches Haftungsrisiko abgedeckt werden kann, wie diese Versicherung im Detail aussieht, wusste er hingegen nicht. Die

Probanden hatten sich über eine Versicherung nie Gedanken gemacht, da sie von Haftungsrisiken keine Kenntnis hatten.

Die Aufklärung bzgl. Absicherungsmöglichkeiten bzw. der Abschluss einer entsprechenden Versicherung sind also erkennbar nicht gängige Praxis in Vereinen.

Hauptkategorie „Kenntnisnahme während des Amtes"

Drei von sechs Probanden hatten bereits während ihrer ehrenamtlichen Tätigkeit Kenntnis von zivilrechtlichen Haftungsrisiken erlangt. Während ein Proband gute Kenntnisse von den Haftungsrisiken erlangt hatte, war bei zwei Probanden die Kenntnislage rudimentär. Ein Problembewusstsein war bei zwei Probanden inzwischen gegeben, jedoch äußerte sich dieses nicht in konkretem Wissen. Ein Proband ignorierte die Risiken und vertraute diesbezüglich vollkommen auf andere Vorstands- und Vereinsmitglieder, denen er zutraute, genauestens zu wissen, was in welcher Situation zu tun ist. Der Proband, der bereits negative Erfahrungen im Ehrenamt gesammelt hatte, hatte keine detaillierte Kenntnis von den Haftungsrisiken gesammelt oder sich entsprechend beraten lassen.

Ergebnisse zu Forschungsfrage 3

Die induktive Kategorienbildung führte bezüglich Forschungsfrage 3 zu folgenden Haupt- und Subkategorien.

Tabelle 5.4: Kategorien zu Forschungsfrage 3

Konsequenzen aus Kenntnis der Risiken
Reaktionen auf Kenntnisnahme

Quelle: eigene Darstellung

Hauptkategorie „Konsequenzen aus Kenntnis der Risiken"

Drei der sechs Interviewpartner hatten vor den Interviews grundsätzlich Kenntnis von Haftungsrisiken. Sie hatten, wie oben aufgezeigt, bereits während ihres ehrenamtlichen Engagements von der grundsätzlichen Möglichkeit der Haftungsrisiken erfahren. Zwei von ihnen hatten daraus jedoch nicht die Konsequenz gezogen, sich detailliert über die Haftungssituation und mögliche Absicherungen gegen diese Risiken zu informieren. Lediglich ein Proband hatte die Konsequenz gezogen, das Amt unter anderem aufgrund der Haftungsrisiken niederzulegen.

Daher liegt der Schluss nahe, dass die beiden Probanden, die an ihren Ämtern festhielten, in ihren Ämtern jeweils so sehr motiviert waren, dass ihnen mögliche Risiken als hinnehmbar erschienen. Der aus dem Amt ausgeschiedene Proband dagegen mochte die möglichen Haftungsrisiken nicht tragen. Das lässt darauf schließen, dass seine Motivation im Ehrenamt nicht ausreichte, um die Sorge vor Haftung zu überwinden. Die Analyse der Interviews bzgl. Forschungsfrage 1 hat ergeben, dass die von diesem Probanden genannten Gründe gegen ein Ehrenamt die Gründe für ein Ehrenamt weit überwogen. Zudem gab dieser Proband an, bereits zuvor Zweifel an seinem Amt gehabt zu haben. Einer der an seinen Ämtern festhaltenden Probanden gab deutlich mehr Gründe für ein Ehrenamt an als dagegen. Von Zweifeln an seinem Amt sprach er an keiner Stelle. Die Tatsache, dass er keine Konsequenzen aus der Kenntnis der Haftungsrisiken zog, spricht dafür, dass er so sehr von seinen Ehrenämtern überzeugt war, dass eine Beendigung für ihn nicht in Frage kam. Für einen anderen an seinen Ämtern festhaltenden Probanden hielten sich die Gründe für und gegen das Ehrenamt die Waage. Er brachte mit seiner wiederholten Aussage, mit seinen Engagements helfen zu wollen, zum Ausdruck, dass es ihm bei jedem einzelnen Engagement um die Sache ging. Von den jeweiligen Projekten war er offensichtlich so überzeugt, dass er die Haftungsrisiken vernachlässigte.

Hauptkategorie „Reaktion auf Kenntnisnahme"

Drei Probanden erfuhren während des Interviews von den Haftungsrisiken und reagierten jeweils mit großer Überraschung. Während einer dieser Probanden erklärte, aufgrund dieser bestehenden Risiken das Amt nicht ohne entsprechende Absicherung weiter ausüben zu wollen, waren die anderen beiden Probanden nach anfänglicher Unsicherheit noch während der Interviews entschlossen, die Ehrenämter auf jeden Fall weiterzuführen.

Zwar überwogen bei dem Probanden, der sofort erklärte, unter diesen Voraussetzungen das Amt nicht weiter auszuführen, die Gründe für ein Ehrenamt jene dagegen. Jedoch äußerte er im Interview, schon vorher Zweifel bzgl. der ehrenamtlichen Tätigkeit gehabt zu haben. Die beiden anderen Probanden hingegen waren deutlich positiver gestimmt, was ehrenamtliche Tätigkeit betrifft. Zweifel an ihrem Einsatz äußerten sie zu keinem Zeitpunkt. Mithin liegt der Schluss nahe, dass eine grundsätzlich positive Haltung zum Ehrenamt allgemein und zum eigenen Ehrenamt insbesondere die Bereitschaft, Risiken einzugehen, stärkt. Zwar gaben diese beiden Probanden auch an, mit ihren Meinungen und Handlungen mitunter konfliktreiche Gespräche geführt zu haben. Dennoch führte diese Situationen zu keinem Zeitpunkt zu Zweifeln am Amt. Dies war bei dem Probanden anders, der sofort seine Niederlegungen des Amtes beabsichtigte.

5.6.2.2. Ergebnisse der Codierung

Für die sich aus der qualitativen Inhaltsanalyse ergebende Hauptkategorie der *Gründe für ein Ehrenamt im Verein* zu Forschungsfrage 1 sowie die Hauptkategorie der *Reaktion/Konsequenz auf die Kenntnisnahme der Haftungsrisiken* zu Forschungsfrage 3 wurde ergänzend eine Codierung vorgenommen. Grundlage für die Codierung waren dabei alle sechs geführten Interviews. Die Codierung führte zu folgenden 14 Codes für die Kategorie.

Tabelle 5.5: Gründe für ein Ehrenamt im Verein

Inhaltliche Interessen	Eigene Interessen	Erfolg	Befriedigung	Helfen wollen	Gutes tun	Berufliche Interessen
Soziale Interessen	Spaß	Mitentscheiden	Gerechtigkeitssinn	Verantwortungsgefühl	Bitte	Sinnhaftigkeit

Quelle: eigene Darstellung

Die Codes, die innerhalb der Kategorie Gründe für ein Ehrenamt im Verein vergeben wurden, wurden in einem nächsten Schritt auf ihr Vorkommen in den einzelnen Interviews der einzelnen Interviewpartner überprüft. Maßgeblich war dabei zunächst die absolute Häufigkeit, mit der die einzelnen Codes bei den Interviews auftreten. Die Häufigkeit der genannten Gründe wurde im nächsten Schritt für jeden Interviewten getrennt ins Verhältnis gesetzt zu allen von ihm vorgetragenen Gründen für das Ehrenamt. Damit sollte der Umstand berücksichtigt werden, dass es mehr oder weniger erzählfreudige Interviewpartner gibt. Vermieden werden sollte somit, dass Kriterien als insgesamt bedeutsam gelten, weil sie besonders häufig genannt wurden, da redefreudigere Interviewpartner die jeweiligen Kriterien wiederholt benennen. Durch das Ins-Verhältnis-Setzen der genannten Gründe jedes einzelnen Interviewten zur Gesamtzahl seiner genannten Gründe entstand ein guter Überblick der individuell bedeutsamsten Gründe für das eigene Ehrenamt.

Für die Hälfte der Probanden sind inhaltliche Interessen unter den zwei subjektiv wichtigsten Gründen. Obwohl fünf von sechs Probanden "Helfen wollen" und "Gutes tun" als Gründe für das ehrenamtliche Engagement genannt haben, spielt dieser Aspekt nach Auswertung mittels qualitativer Inhaltsanalyse und Codierung nur bei einem Drittel der Probanden eine übergeordnete Rolle. Bei allen anderen werden diese allgemein bekannten und oft als altruistisch bezeichneten Gründe von anderen Gründen überlagert. Bei ebenfalls der Hälfte der Interviewten zeigt sich, dass Erfolg/Befriedigung einer der zwei bedeutsamsten Gründe für ihr Ehrenamt ist.

Im Rahmen einer eher explorativen Betrachtung der genannten Gründe ist erkennbar, dass das Mitentscheiden für diejenigen, die beruflich in führenden Positionen sind/waren, keinerlei Bedeutung hat. Diejenigen Probanden, für die Mitentscheiden sehr wichtig ist, hatten beruflich keine Führungsposition inne.

Für die Kategorien *Konsequenzen aus der Kenntnis der Risiken* bzw. *Reaktion auf Kenntnisnahme* im Rahmen der Forschungsfragen 2 und 3 ergab die Codierung unter anderem folgende Kriterien:

- Verärgerung über Unkenntnis
- Verärgerung über eigene Naivität
- mangelnde Bereitschaft, Risiken zu tragen
- unveränderte Bereitschaft, Risiken zu tragen
- eingeschränkte Bereitschaft, Risiken zu tragen
- Unsicherheit
- Verkennen der Risiken
- Bedingungen für künftige Ehrenämter

In der Betrachtung der Variablen *Reaktionen auf die Kenntnis der Haftungsrisiken* in den Ausprägungen *uneingeschränkte Bereitschaft zum Ehrenamt* und *mangelnde Bereitschaft* in Kombination mit der Variablen *Gründe für ein Ehrenamt* stellte sich heraus, dass die Kombination von *uneingeschränkter Bereitschaft* und *inhaltliches Interesse* für das Ehrenamt sowie *Erfolg/Befriedigung* und *uneingeschränkte Bereitschaft* am häufigsten vorkommt.

Dies deutet darauf hin, dass diejenigen Ehrenamtlichen, die mit ihrer Tätigkeit inhaltliche Interessen verfolgen, eine größere Bereitschaft zur Übernahme von Risiken haben. Das Verspüren von großer Erfüllung/Befriedigung bei einer erfolgreichen ehrenamtlichen Tätigkeit, führt ebenfalls zu einer verstärkten Bereitschaft zum Engagement.

Zwei Interviewpartner, die ein Fortführen der Ehrenämter ohne entsprechende Absicherung ausschlossen, gaben an, "erschreckt" bzw. "verärgert" über die Unkenntnis bzgl. möglicher Haftungsrisiken zu sein.

5.7. Typenbildung

Nach der Analyse waren die Ergebnisse zu systematisieren. Hierfür eignete sich das Modell der empirisch begründeten Typenbildung.

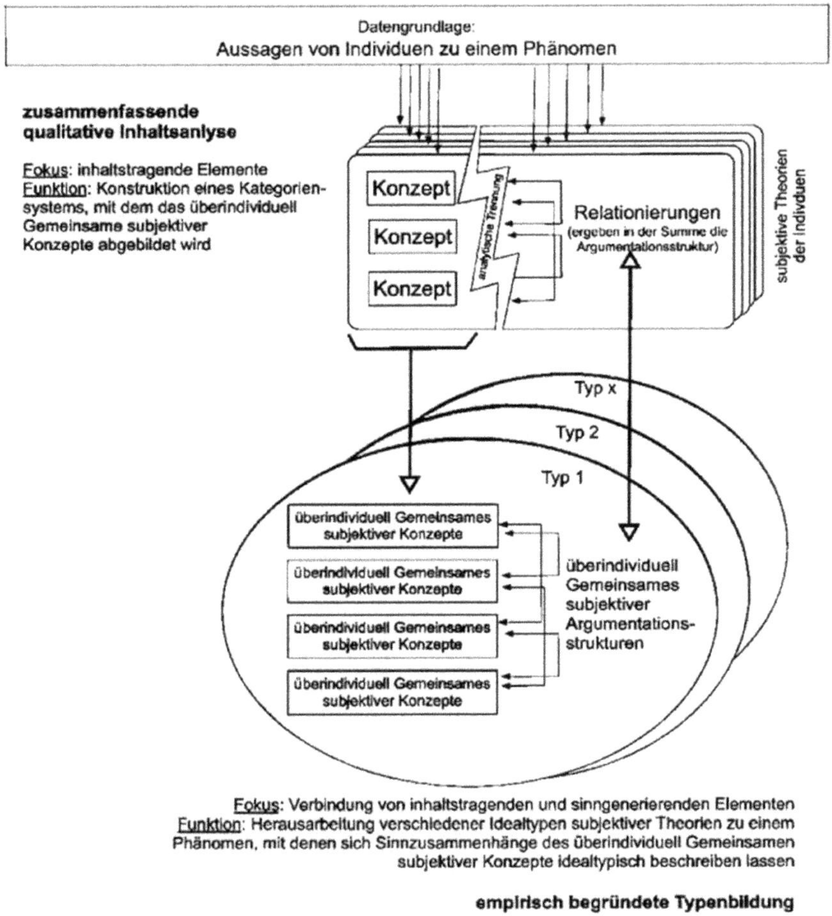

Abbildung 5.1: Empirisch begründete Typenbildung
Quelle: Lang and Ruesch Schweizer, 2020, Abs. 15.

Ziel dieses methodischen Verfahrens ist es, aus den Inhalten der Interviews für die einzelnen Interviewten einen "gemeinsamen Nenner" herauszuarbeiten, mittels dessen die einzelnen bedeutsamen inhaltlichen Elemente "überindividuell" und komprimiert dargestellt werden können (vgl. Lang et al., 2020, S. 13). Auf der Grundlage von empirischem Datenmaterial werden somit Hypothesen über Typen-(Gruppen) generiert, die über das zugrundeliegende Datenmaterial hinausgehen (vgl. Lang et al., 2020, S. 29).

In der hier vorliegenden Forschung wurde das Modell zur empirisch begründeten Typenbildung auf die Aussagen der sechs Interviewten bzgl. ihrer Motivation zur Ausübung ihrer Ehrenämter und ihre Haltung zu möglichen Haftungsrisiken angewandt.

Die durchgeführte qualitative Inhaltsanalyse hatte zur Bildung von Kategorien geführt. Die Darstellung der individuellen Konzepte wurde auf die jeweils drei wichtigsten Gründe für das Ehrenamt sowie die Reaktion auf die Kenntnis(-nahme) von möglichen Haftungsrisiken reduziert. Daraus ergaben sich für die sechs Interviewten die folgenden Konzepte:

Proband 1 ist erfolgsorientiert, mit seinem Engagement den Bitten von anderen Vereinsmitgliedern gefolgt und möchte helfen bzw. dem Club etwas zurückgeben. Seine Beweggründe sind ihm hinsichtlich der starken Erfolgsorientierung nicht bewusst. Auf die Kenntnis von Haftungsrisiken reagiert er mit Niederlegung des Ehrenamtes.

Proband 2 folgt mit ihrem Ehrenamt einem großen Verantwortungsgefühl, sie sucht und erfährt Befriedigung durch eine erfolgreiche Arbeit in ihrem Amt. Sie möchte helfen, lässt sich dabei aber auch stark von positivem Feedback und der Möglichkeit mitzuentscheiden leiten. Sie reagiert mit einer unverminderten Bereitschaft, das Amt und die damit verbundenen Haftungsrisiken weiter zu betreiben.

Proband 3 ist von dem Wunsch, Gutes zu tun sowie dem großen Bedürfnis, bestimmte Inhalte voranzutreiben, geleitet. Sein Engagement ist zudem abhängig davon, dass er einen persönlichen Bezug zu den Personen hat, mit denen er das Ehrenamt ausübt. Auf die Kenntnis von Haftungsrisiken reagiert er vordergründig mit eingeschränkter Bereitschaft, das Amt weiterzuführen. Tatsächlich signalisiert er aber, bei entsprechendem inhaltlichem Interesse auch wieder Ehrenämter zu übernehmen.

Proband 4 verfolgt mit seinen Ehrenämtern überwiegend eigene, inhaltliche und berufliche Interessen. Diese Motive sind ihm auch bewusst. Auf die Kenntnisnahme von möglichen Haftungsrisiken reagiert er mit einer unverminderten Bereitschaft, die Ämter weiter zu betreiben.

Proband 5 verfolgt mit seinen Ehrenämtern ebenfalls überwiegend inhaltliche und berufliche Interessen, wobei er dabei auch stark erfolgsorientiert ist. Auch ihm sind seine Beweggründe bewusst. Auf die Kenntnis von Haftungsrisiken während seiner Ämter hat er mit unverminderter Bereitschaft und dem Fortsetzen der Ämter reagiert.

Proband 6 verfolgt stark eigene Interessen, derer sie sich nicht durchgängig bewusst ist. Ihr ist ein gewisses Mitspracherecht wichtig und die verfolgten inhaltlichen Interessen werden mitunter unbewusst von eigenen Interessen überlagert. Sie reagiert auf die Kenntnisnahme von der Haftung mit der Weigerung, unter den bestehenden Bedingungen das Ehrenamt fortzuführen.

Das *überindividuell Gemeinsame* von Proband 4 und Proband 5 ist eine extrinsische Motivation, derer sich beide auch bewusst sind. Sie wägen Vorteile und Nachteile, die mit ihrer Tätigkeit verbunden sind, ab und kommen zu dem Ergebnis, dass die Haftungsrisiken hinnehmbar sind.

Das *überindividuell Gemeinsame* von Proband 1 und Proband 6 ist eine extrinsische Motivation, derer sie sich nicht bewusst sind. Die Haftungsrisiken stehen für sie in keinem hinnehmbaren Verhältnis zu den Vorteilen, die sie aus den Ämtern ziehen.

Proband 2 und Proband 3 *gemeinsam* ist, dass sie überwiegend intrinsisch motiviert sind, jedoch mit extrinsischen Zügen. Ihre Motivation zum Ehrenamt hat ein höheres Gewicht als die damit verbundenen Risiken.

Abschließend lassen sich drei Typen unter den Ehrenamtlichen identifizieren:

Typ A: überwiegend extrinsisch motiviert; Bewusstsein der extrinsischen Motivationslage; große Bereitschaft zur Übernahme von Risiken.

Typ B: überwiegend extrinsisch motiviert; kein Bewusstsein von der tatsächlichen Motivation; keine Bereitschaft zur Übernahme von Risiken.

Typ C: überwiegend intrinsisch motiviert; großer Bereitschaft zur Übernahme von Risiken.

5.8. Zusammenfassung der Ergebnisse und Thesen

Aus der qualitativen Inhaltsanalyse ergeben sich zu Forschungsfrage 1 die Hauptkategorien „Gründe für ein Ehrenamt", „Gründe gegen ein Ehrenamt" und „Verständnis von Ehrenamt". Die Gründe für ein Ehrenamt im Vorstand eines Vereins sind sehr individuell. Alle Probanden gaben an, mit ihrem Engagement helfen zu wollen. Allen Probanden war es wichtig, mit ihrer Tätigkeit etwas Sinnvolles zu bewirken. Erfolg ist ein weiteres Kriterium, welches ebenfalls allen wichtig war.

Ein wesentliches Ergebnis der vorliegenden Forschung ist, dass es eine Diskrepanz zwischen den selbst wahrgenommenen Gründen für das jeweilige Ehrenamt und den tatsächlich vorliegenden Gründen gibt, die sich zum Teil erst im Rahmen der vorgenommenen Codierung identifizieren ließen. Zwei Probanden gaben im Interview dieselben Interessen an, die sich auch aus der

Codierung ergeben haben. Vier Probanden waren sich ihrer eigenen Motive nicht umfänglich bewusst.

Die Hauptkategorien „keine Kenntnis vom Haftungsrisiko“, „Kenntnis von D&O Versicherung“ und „Kenntnisnahme während eines Ehrenamtes“ zu Forschungsfrage 2 zeigen, dass drei Probanden keinerlei Kenntnis von irgendwelchen Haftungsrisiken hatten. Ein Proband von diesen Dreien hatte keine Kenntnis, obwohl er schon seit vielen Jahren in verschiedenen Ehrenämtern tätig war. Ein Proband hatte trotz einer grundsätzlichen Kenntnis, dass Haftungsrisiken bestehen, nur rudimentäre Kenntnisse von den tatsächlichen Risiken. Kein Proband kannte allerdings die sog. D&O Versicherung für Organe von beispielsweise eingetragenen Vereinen.

Die Hauptkategorien zu Forschungsfrage 3 sind „Konsequenzen aus der Kenntnis der Risiken“ und „Reaktionen auf die Kenntnisnahme“ während des Interviews. Die beiden oben genannten Probanden, die zumindest wussten, dass es ein Haftungsproblem in irgendeiner Form geben kann, hatten hieraus keine weiteren Konsequenzen gezogen. Der Proband, der sich von einem Rechtsanwalt hatte beraten lassen, zog die Konsequenz, das Ehrenamt niederzulegen. Zwei Probanden, die im Interview von möglichen Risiken erfuhren, waren zunächst verunsichert, erklärten jedoch noch im Interview ihr Ehrenamt nicht niederlegen zu wollen. Eine Probandin war derart verunsichert, dass sie angibt, sofort eine Vorstandssitzung einberufen und ohne Versicherung keine Fortsetzung des Amtes zu wollen.

Eine an die qualitative Inhaltsanalyse anschließende Typenbildung führte zu folgenden Typen: Lediglich zwei Interviewten war die Verknüpfung ihrer inhaltlichen, z. T. auch damit verbundenen beruflichen Interessen mit ihrem Ehrenamt bewusst. Diese Personen werden im Rahmen der empirisch begründeten Typenbildung als Typ A bezeichnet. Überwiegend befanden sich die befragten Ehrenamtlichen in einer Position, in der sie sich mehr oder weniger verpflichtet sahen, der Gesellschaft bzw. Teilen der Gesellschaft zu helfen und damit etwas Gutes zu tun. Das sind die Gründe, die sie für sich selbst sahen und auch nach außen kommunizierten. Faktisch wurden in einigen Fällen diese in der Gesellschaft weit verbreiteten, akzeptierten und auch positiv bewerteten Gründe von anderen Gründen überlagert. Dieses Umstandes waren sich die Interviewpartner zumindest nicht im kompletten Ausmaß bewusst. Personen dieses Phänomens werden dem Typ B zugeordnet. Diejenigen, die überwiegend intrinsisch motiviert sind, sind dem Typ C zugeordnet.

Aus den Ergebnissen der vorliegenden Forschung wurden die folgenden Thesen generiert:

These 1: Ein Ehrenamtlicher, der überwiegend extrinsisch motiviert ist und sich dessen auch bewusst ist, hat eine größere Bereitschaft zur Übernahme von Haftungsrisiken als ein Ehrenamtlicher, der überwiegend extrinsisch motiviert ist und sich dessen nicht bewusst ist.

These 2: Überwiegend intrinsisch motivierte Ehrenamtliche zeichnen sich durch eine große Bereitschaft zur Übernahme von Haftungsrisiken aus.

Handlungsempfehlungen

Empfehlung 1: NPOs, die auf der Suche nach neuen Ehrenamtlichen sind, sollten sich des Umstandes bewusst sein, dass die in vorab geführten Gesprächen vor Eintritt in die Organisation angegebenen Gründe für ihr Interesse an einem Ehrenamt in vielen Fällen nicht die wahren Gründe der Bewerber sind. NPOs bzw. Vereine sollten sich daher tiefer mit den Motiven zur Ehrenamtsübernahme auseinandersetzten, um geeignete Kandidaten anzusprechen. Zudem sollte eine Aufklärung zu den bestehenden Haftungsrisiken erfolgen.

Empfehlung 2: Auch in Vereinen, in denen Haftungsrisiken nicht bekannt sind, kann die Typisierung zur Gewinnung und Bindung von Ehrenamtlichen genutzt werden.

Typ A, der eine genaue Vorstellung von dem hat, was er von dem Ehrenamt erwartet, kann in seinen individuellen Erwartungen befriedigt werden. Wenn es sich um berufliche Erwartungen handelt, ist oft schon die Übernahme des Amtes an sich eine Möglichkeit, sich weitere Karriereperspektiven zu schaffen.

Typ B ist am schwierigsten zu identifizieren, da er seine eigenen Motive nicht kennt, sich ggf. hinsichtlich seiner wahren Motive sogar selbst etwas vormacht. Wie sich aus der Studie gezeigt hat, ist Anerkennung, positives Feedback und eine soziale Komponente für alle drei Typen wichtig. Daher sollte an diesen Aspekten angesetzt werden.

Insbesondere hinsichtlich Typ C ist eine starke Organisationskultur anzustreben. Eine starke Organisationskultur liegt dann vor, wenn u. a. bei den Ehrenamtlichen Klarheit über Werte und Normen herrscht und diese die jeweiligen Werte und Normen verinnerlicht haben.

Empfehlung 3: Ehrenamtliche sollten mit einer D&O- Versicherung gegen Haftungsrisiken abgesichert werden.

Empfehlung 4: Da grundsätzlich intrinsisch motivierte Ehrenamtliche einfacher an die NPO zu binden sind, sollte der Fokus auf diese Personengruppe gelegt werden. NPOs sollten ihren Tätigkeitsbereich klar definieren und

kommunizieren, sodass die am Ehrenamt Interessierten anhand der Inhalte die Entscheidung, für die eine oder die andere NPO treffen können.
Die Vereine sollten mehr über die Tätigkeiten von Ehrenamtlichen informieren und Weiterbildungsmöglichkeiten nutzen.

Empfehlung 5: Vereine sollten besser über Rechte auf Ehrenamtspauschalen und Kostenerstattungen aufklären.

Empfehlung 6: Die Zusammensetzung von Vorständen ist stets im Auge zu behalten und hier auf eine Kombination unterschiedlicher Persönlichkeiten und sich fachlich ergänzender Personen Wert zu legen. Es bewährt sich erkennbar, wenn Vorstandsmitglieder zunächst bei ihrer Tätigkeit durch erfahrene Vorstandsmitglieder begleitet werden, bevor sie eigenverantwortlich das Vorstandsamt übernehmen.

Empfehlung 7: Vereine sollten ein verstärktes Augenmerk auf die Amtsübergaben beim Vorstandswechsel legen. Eine Möglichkeit besteht in einer durch Steuerberater oder Wirtschaftsprüfer begleiteten Übergabe.

Literatur

Adams, J. (1963). Towards an Understanding of Inequity. *The Journal of Abnormal and Social Psychology*, 67(5), pp. 422–436. https://doi.org/10.1037/h0040968

Anheier, H. K. & Seibel, W. (2004). The Nonprofit Sector in Germany. Between State, Economy and Society. *German Studies Review*. https://doi.org/10.2307/1433608

Bock, M. (1992). „Das halbstrukturierte-leitfadenorientierte Tiefeninterview". Theorie und Praxis der Methode am Beispiel von Paarinterviews. In J. H. P. Hoffmeyer-Zlotnik (Hrsg.), VS Verlag für Sozialwissenschaften eBooks (S. 90–109). Springer VS. https://doi.org/10.1007/978-3-322-90092-0_4

Breuer, C. & Feiler, S. (2019): Sportvereine in Deutschland: Organisationen und Personen. Sportentwicklungsbericht für Deutschland 2017/2018-Teil 1, Bundesinstitut für Sportwissenschaft.

Breyter, M. (2022). *Agile Product and Project Management*. Apress. https://doi.org/10.1007/978-1-4842-8200-7

Bruhn, M. (2013). *Qualitätsmanagement für Nonprofit-Organisationen*. SpringerGabler. https://doi.org/10.1007/978-3-658-00354-8

Bund & Länder | Parlament Österreich (O. D.). https://www.parlament.gv.at/PERK/BOE/PR/index.shtml

Bundesministerium für Justiz, Österreich (2017): *Zivil- und strafrechtliche Aspekte zum Vereinswesen. Vereinsenquete 2017*. Mai 2017

Davis, J., Schoorman, F. D. & Donaldson, L. (1997). Toward a Stewardship Theory of Management. *Academy of Management Review*, 22(1), p. 20. https://doi.org/10.2307/259223

Dörner, H. (2019): *§ 31 a BGB Haftung von Organmitgliedern und besonderen Vertretern.* In: Bürgerliches Gesetzbuch Handkommentar (Schriftleitung Reiner Schulze), 10. Auflage, Nomos.

Ebers, M. & Gotsch, W. (2014). Institutionenökonomische Theorien der Organisation. In A. Kieser & M. Ebers (Hrsg.), *Organisationstheorien* (S. 206–224). Kohlhammer.

Frey, B. S. & Jegen, R. (2001). Motivation Crowding Theory. *Journal of Economic Surveys*. https://doi.org/10.1111/1467641900150

Helmig, B. & Boenigk, S. (2019): *Nonprofit Management.* https://doi.org/10.15358/9783800651801

Herzberg, F., Mausner, B. & Bloch Snyderman, B. (2010). *The Motivation to Work.* https://doi.org/10.4324/9781315124827

Hippel, von, T. (2005). Typologie der Nonprofit-Organisationen. In K. J. Hopt, T. v. Hippel & W. R. Walz (Hrsg.), *Nonprofit-Organisation in Recht, Wirtschaft und Gesellschaft.* Mohr Siebeck.

IFES, Institut für empirische Sozialforschung (2016). *Freiwilligenengagement – Bevölkerungsbefragung 2016 – Studienbericht.* Studie im Auftrag des Bundesministeriums für Arbeit, Soziales und Konsumentenschutz, Wien. https://www.nachhaltigkeit.steiermark.at/cms/dokumente/12621817_99560887/07cb248a/bericht_freiwilligenengagement_2016.pdf

Kreitner, R./Kinicki, A. (2013): *Organizational Behavior.* 10. Auflage, McGraw-Hill/Irwin.

Land Nordrhein-Westfalen, Staatskanzlei (Hrsg.) (2020): *Sicherheit im Ehrenamt. Versicherungsschutz für freiwilliges Engagement* https://www.land.nrw/sites/default/files/asset/document/faltblatt_sicherheit_im_ehrenamt_stand_241017_0.pdf

Lang, S. & Ruesch Schweizer, C. (2020). Idealtypische subjektive Theorien – eine theoretisch fundierte Konkretisierung der Kombination von zusammenfassender qualitativer Inhaltsanalyse und empirisch begründeter Typenbildung. Forum: Qualitative Sozialforschung (FQS), Januar 2020, 21(1), Art. 18.

Leuschner, L. (2014): Das Haftungsprivileg der §§ 31a, 31b BGB. *Neue Zeitschrift für Gesellschaftsrecht (NZG)*, 2014.

Leuschner, L. (2018): *§ 31 a BGB. In* F. J. Säcker, R. Rixecker, H. Oetker & B. Limperg (Hrsg.), *Münchener Kommentar zum Bürgerlichen Gesetzbuch.* 8. Auflage, C. H. Beck.

Lichtsteiner, H., Gmür, M. & Giroud, C. & Schauer, R. (2020). *Das Freiburger Management-Modell für Nonprofit-Organisationen.* Haupt.

Mayerhofer, H. & von Eckardstein, D. (2001). Personalstrategien für Ehrenamtliche. Zeitschrift für Personalforschung (ZfP), *3/2001.* https://doi.org/10.1177/239700220101500302

Mayring, P. (2020). Introduction: Foundations of Qualitative Content Analysis. In *QCAmap Step by Step – A Software Handbook.* https://dx.doi.org/10.17169/fqs-20.3.3343

Mroß, M. D. (2009). *Personale Arbeit in Nonprofit Organisationen: Grundlagen – Theorie – Ökonomik.* Akademische Verlagsgemeinschaft München.

Nowotny, C. & Fida, S. (2007): *Rechtliche Gestaltungsformen für NPOs.* In R. Simsa, M. Meyer & C. Badelt (Hrsg.), *Handbuch der Nonprofit-Organisationen. Strukturen und Management*). 4. Auflage, Schäffer-Poeschel Verlag.

Nowotny, C. (2013). Rechtliche Gestaltungsformen für NPOs. In R. Simsa, M. Meyer & C. Badelt (Hrsg.), *Handbuch der Nonprofit-Organisationen. Strukturen und Management.* Schäffer-Poeschel.

Pennerstorfer, A., Schneider, U. & Badelt, C. (2013). Der Nonprofit Sektor in Österreich. In R. Simsa, M. Meyer & C. Badelt (Hrsg.), *Handbuch der Nonprofit-Organisation: Strukturen und Management.* Schäffer-Poeschel.

Republik Österreich, Parlament (2019): https://www.parlament.gv.at/PERK/BOE/PR/index.shtml

Schwarz, P., Purtschert, R., Giroud, C. & Schauer, R. (1995). *Das Freiburger Management-Modell für Nonprofit-Organisationen.* Haupt.

Simon, Herbert A. (1991). Organizations and Markets. *Journal of Economic Perspectives, 5,* American Economic Association.

Simsa, R. (2001). Einflussstrategien von Nonprofit Organisationen: Ausprägungen und Konsequenzen für das Personalmanagement. *Zeitschrift Fur Personalforschung, 15*(3), 284–305. https://doi.org/10.1177/239700220101500305

Simsa, R. (2003): Einflussstrategien von Nonprofit Organisationen: Ausprägungen und Konsequenzen für das Personalmanagement. In D. v. Eckardstein & H. G. Ridder (Hrsg.), *Personalmanagement als Gestaltungsaufgabe im Nonprofit und Public Management* Rainer Hampp.

Statista (2019a). Der deutsche Freiwilligensurvey 2019, Daten nach Bundesamt für Familie, Senioren, Frauen und Jugend (BMFSFJ).

Statista. (2019b). *Daten nach Bundesamt für Familie, Senioren, Frauen und Jugend (BMFSFJ), n. d. In welchem organisatorischen Rahmen üben Sie Ihre freiwillige Tätigkeit aus? Freiwilliges Engagement–Organisationsform.*

Suchanek, A. (2021). *Definition: Subsidiarität*. Gabler Wirtschaftslexikon. https://wirtschaftslexikon.gabler.de/definition/subsidiaritaet-44920

Taylor, F. W. (1913) *Die Grundsätze wissenschaftlicher Betriebsführung*. Beltz .

Winheller, S. (2010). Nonprofit-Organisationen in Deutschland und in den USA. *Zeitschrift für Stiftungs- und Vereinswesen (ZStV), 2010*. Nomos.

Zimmer, A. (2001). Der deutsche Nonprofit-Sektor – Ein empirischer Beitrag zur Bedeutung von Nonprofit-Organisationen in der Bundesrepublik Deutschland. In H. Kötz, P. Rawert, K. Schmidt & R. Walz (Hrsg.), *Non Profit Law Yearbook 2001*. Heymann.

Zimmer, A. & Priller, E. (2007). *Gemeinnützige Organisationen im gesellschaftlichen Wandel-Ergebnisse der Dritte-Sektor-Forschung*. Springer VS. https://doi.org/10.1007/9783531907482

Zimmer, A., Priller, E. & Anheier, H. K. (2013). Der Nonprofit-Sektor in Deutschland. In R. Simsa, M. Meyer & C. Badelt (Hrsg.), *Handbuch der Nonprofit Organisation. Strukturen und Management*. Schäffer-Poeschel.

Norbert Klein

6. Mit Zielen agil führen: Innovative Anwendung der OKR-Methode in einer Sparkasse

Zusammenfassung: Zur Erreichung ihrer Unternehmensziele nutzen Sparkassen, wie alle Banken und Unternehmen, Systeme zur Zielsteuerung. Oftmals sind die Systeme mit Beurteilungssystemen für die Mitarbeitenden verbunden und werden jährlich, beispielsweise im Rahmen von Jahresgesprächen, erörtert.

Aber sind diese Systeme noch geeignet, in einer inzwischen sehr dynamischen Welt, die Beiträge der einzelnen Mitarbeitenden zur Erreichung der Unternehmensziele zu steuern? Hier bietet die OKR-Methode (O steht für Objectives, KR steht für Key Results) eine mögliche, innovative Alternative.

In der untersuchten, mittelgroßen Sparkasse wurde die OKR-Methode vor drei Jahren eingeführt. Nach den ersten Durchläufen wurde deutlich, dass eine Modifikation notwendig war. Hierzu hat der Autor, zusammen mit einer weiteren Führungskraft der Untersuchungssparkasse, die Ergebnisse aus den Rückschauen ausgewertet und hiernach ein Konzept zu einer angepassten Anwendung der OKR-Methode für die Sparkasse entwickelt.

Die Erkenntnisse sind nicht nur für Sparkassen, sondern für alle Unternehmen interessant, die sich mit der OKR-Methode auseinandersetzen.

Schlagworte: Objectives, Key Results, Sparkasse, Innovation, Ziel, Zielsteuerung, Führung, Führungsinstrumente, Unternehmenssteuerung, Review, Retro, Weekly, Aufgabensteuerung

6.1. Problemstellung

Der vorliegende Beitrag behandelt das aktuelle Thema der Zielsteuerung in Unternehmen mit eher konservativem Umfeld. Die Thematik wird am Beispiel der Führung und Zielsteuerung in einer Sparkasse dargelegt. In der heutigen Zeit stoßen in Unternehmen mit konservativem Umfeld traditionelle Zielvereinbarungen an ihre Grenzen und sind überholt. Derartige Zielsteuerungssysteme wurden bisher einerseits genutzt, um (Vertriebs-) Ziele zu verteilen und deren Erreichung zu kontrollieren. Andererseits dienten sie der Leistungsbewertung von Mitarbeitern. Im Rahmen eines Führungskräfte-Workshops haben die Führungskräfte der an der Untersuchung beteiligten Sparkasse ihre Unzufriedenheit mit dem bisherigen Zielsteuerungssystem zum Ausdruck gebracht. Die Gründe für die

Unzufriedenheit waren vielfältig. Zum einen wurde die Zielsteuerung als zu starr und die Verbindung zum Bewertungssystem als nicht gerecht wahrgenommen. Eine Alternative fand sich mit der Idee einer agilen Zielsteuerung mittels OKR, welche moderne Unternehmen auf der Basis von John Doerrs Konzept seit einiger Zeit einsetzen (Doerr, 2018).

Vor diesem Hintergrund wurde im Rahmen der Untersuchung folgenden Forschungsfragen nachgegangen:

Forschungsfrage 1: Inwieweit ist die OKR-Methode für die Zielsteuerung und als Führungsinstrument in einer Sparkasse geeignet?

Forschungsfrage 2: In welcher Form kann die OKR-Methode in einer Sparkasse angewandt werden?

Um die Leser an das Thema heranzuführen, wird im folgenden Abschnitt dieses Artikels der theoretische Hintergrund der Methoden zu Zielsteuerungssystemen dargestellt. Im ersten Schritt dieser Ausführungen werden zunächst die theoretischen Grundlagen der Managementmethode mittels „Objectives“ und „Key Results“ (OKR) sowie die Anwendung der Methode vorgestellt. Im zweiten Schritt werden dem Leser darüber hinaus alternative Ideen und Methoden zur Zielsteuerung aufgezeigt. Anschließend wird die konkrete Anwendung in der untersuchten Sparkasse vorgestellt. Der folgende Abschnitt enthält diesbezüglich eine Darstellung der besonderen Bedingungen der mittelgroßen Sparkasse. Dabei wird zunächst auf die Notwendigkeit von geeigneten Zielsystemen und hiernach sowohl auf die unterschiedlichen Organisationseinheiten als auch auf die Herausforderungen in der Anwendung eingegangen. Sodann werden ein eigens für die Sparkasse entwickeltes Konzept mit Lösungsansätzen und die adaptierte Ausgestaltung einer agilen Zielsteuerung als Führungsinstrument auf Basis der OKR-Philosophie vorgestellt. Im Rahmen der Forschung wurden hier die bereits im Rahmen der Rückschauen aus der Praxisanwendung gelieferten Erkenntnisse durch eine vergleichende Analyse bewertet. Abschließend werden die Erkenntnisse der Arbeit bis hin zu Handlungsempfehlungen zusammengefasst.

6.2. OKR – eine agile Methode zur Zielsteuerung

Alle Unternehmen sind dazu angehalten, zur Erreichung ihrer Unternehmensziele, die sie regelmäßig formulieren und in ihren Strategien festhalten, auf die einzelnen Organisationseinheiten zu übertragen. Eine Herausforderung besteht darin, die Unternehmensziele hinreichend konkret für die einzelnen Teams und ihre Mitglieder zu konkretisieren und handhabbar zu machen. Hier kommt eine moderne Methode ins Spiel, die aus dem Silicon Valley langsam auch in Europa und Deutschland Einzug hält: Objectives and Key Results (OKR). (Praz, 2022)

Als Schöpfer des agilen Zielmanagementsystems OKR gilt Andrew Grove, der 1971 bei Intel diese neue Methode einführte und nutzte (changement, 2022). OKR ist ein Steuerungs- und Führungsmodell, auf das John Doerr 1999 aufmerksam machte, indem er es für Google adaptierte und nutzte, um Ziele zu entwickeln, zu messen und umzusetzen. Er half Google mittels OKR in der Gründungsphase, die Entwicklungs- und Wachstumsziele zu steuern und diente so auch als Vorbild für zahlreiche andere Unternehmen (Doerr, 2018). Beispielsweise Edeka, Daimler oder die Deutsche Telekom nutzen bereits OKR (die.agilen, 2022). Studien zeigen, dass agile Managementmethoden – wie OKR – in der Praxis Zuspruch finden (Becker et al., 2020).

6.3. Funktionsweise der Methode

Das OKR-Modell ist ein zyklischer Prozess, der mit Hilfe von Objectives und Key Results Mitarbeiter und Führungskräfte dabei unterstützt, zusammenzuarbeiten und ihre Bemühungen zu fokussieren, um einen messbaren Beitrag für die Erreichung der Unternehmensziele zu leisten. (Niven & Lamorte, 2016)

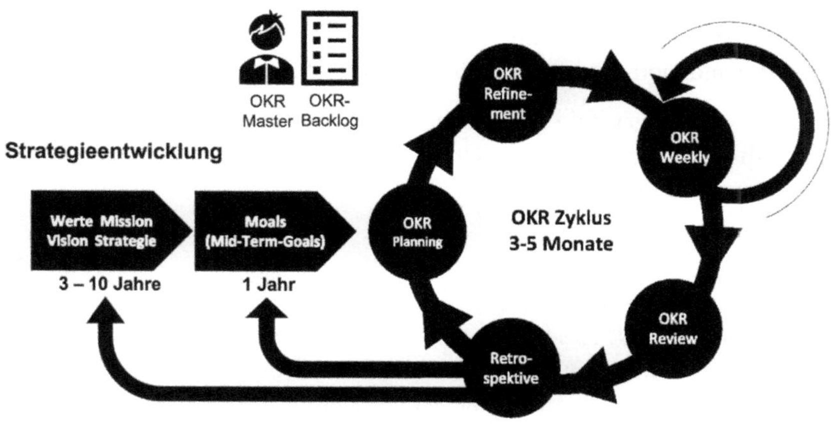

Abbildung 6.1: Darstellung des OKR-Regelkreises
Quelle: Wozny (2021)

Der OKR-Regelkreis ist ein agiler Prozess. Aufbauend auf dem normativen Rahmen des Unternehmens werden jährlich sogenannte Moals (Mid-Term-Goals) mit einer Gültigkeit von einem Jahr entwickelt. Daran schließen sich für ein Jahr drei bis vier OKR-Zyklen von drei bis fünf Monaten an. Ein Zyklus startet mit dem sogenannten Planning. Es folgen wöchentlich oder 14-tägig Weeklys. Der Zyklus wird dann mit dem Review/Retro beendet und es folgt der Start des nächsten Zyklus, wiederum mit dem Planning. (Wozny, 2021)

Die einzelnen Elemente des OKR-Modells werden in der Folge in ihrem Charakter beschrieben.

6.3.1. Zielelement *Moal*

Nicht zwingend notwendig, aber oft hilfreich, ist die Nutzung von Mid-Term-Goals (Moals) (changement, 2022). In diese Zielart fließen Elemente aus dem normativen Rahmen des Unternehmens, in der Regel bestehend aus Werten, Vision, Mission, und Strategie, ein. Moals dienen somit als Bindeglied zwischen der normativen bzw. der strategischen Ebene und dem Zielsystem des Unternehmens. Sie gelten für ein Jahr und bilden für diesen Zeitraum die Jahresschwerpunkte des Zielsystems. (Wozny, 2021)

Geeignete Moals könnten folgende Anforderungen erfüllen:

- übergeordnet (abstrakt und nicht messbar)
- innerhalb eines Jahres erreichbar
- qualitativ
- großer Handlungsspielraum
- positiv und motivierend mit Verb formuliert (Weber, 2019)

Diese Anforderungen sind nicht zwingend. Ebenso sind Moals nicht zwingend erforderlich. Dennoch geben sie Orientierung zur Ableitung von „Objectives“. (changement, 2022)

6.3.2. Zielelement *Objectives*

Für jeweils einen Zyklus werden, ggf. aus den Moals abgeleitet, Objectives („Os“) gebildet. Diese Ziele beschreiben, *was* erreicht werden soll und werden daher auch als „Was-Ziele“ bezeichnet. Objectives können von „oben“, also von Teamleitern oder aus der Hierarchie heraus über die Kaskade vorgegeben, oder auch aus dem Team heraus – unter der Moderation der Teamleitung – entwickelt werden. Sie gelten dann für das gesamte Team. In der Literatur wird dort (variierend durch Art der Aufgabe, Art des Teams etc.) ein Mix aus ca. 60 % von oben und ca. 40 % von unten als geeignet angesehen. Ebenso ist es möglich, dass unterschiedliche Teams gemeinsame Objectives bilden. (Kudernatsch, 2019)

Als Anforderungen an ein geeignetes Objective können angesehen werden:

- übergeordnetes „Was-Ziel“ (nicht detailliert und nicht messbar)
- innerhalb eines Zyklus umsetzbar (im Gegensatz zum Moal)
- genügend Handlungsspielraum
- positiv und motivierend mit einem Verb formuliert (Weber, 2019)

Das Team verfügt pro Zyklus über etwa zwei bis vier Objectives, auf deren Erreichung die Teammitglieder mit eigenen Beitragszielen, so genannte Key Results, hinwirken. (Niven & Lamorte, 2016)

6.3.3. Zielelement *Key Result*

Auch Key Results (KRs) für den jeweiligen Zyklus werden von jedem einzelnen Teammitglied als Beitrag für ein oder mehrere Objectives formuliert. Ein Key Result beschreibt, was sich ein Teammitglied konkret für den jeweiligen Zyklus vornimmt, also wie bzw. was es zur Zielerreichung beiträgt (Niven & Lamorte, 2016). Daher kann ein Key Result auch als „Wie-Ziel“ bezeichnet werden (Wozny, 2021).

Für geeignete Key Results gelten (im Gegensatz zu Objectives) allgemeine Anforderungen an Zielformulierungen, beispielsweise nach dem SMART-Modell. Geeignete Anforderungen an ein Key Result können demnach sein:

- (S) spezifisch
- (M) messbar
- (A) attraktiv
- (R) realistisch
- (T) terminiert – ergibt sich aus dem Zyklusende (Wozny, 2021)

Die Beziehung zwischen den Zieltypen im OKR-Modell ist im Folgenden in Form des Zielmodells dargestellt:

Abbildung 6.2: Zielsystem für die Methode OKR

Quelle: eigene Darstellung

Zur Veranschaulichung seien aus der Untersuchungssparkasse für die Zielformulierung von Moals über Objectives hin zu Key Results aufgezeigt:

- *Moal:* *„Wir erhöhen den Digitalisierungsgrad unserer Sparkasse!"*
- *Objective* *„Wir bauen unsere technischen Möglichkeiten in unserer Abteilung aus!"*
- *Key Result:* *„Ich erstelle eine digitale Musterakte!"*

6.3.4. Prozesselement *Zyklus*

Die Laufzeit eines Zyklus beträgt in der Regel zwischen drei und fünf Monaten, abhängig von der Aufgabenstellung. Meist dauert ein Zyklus drei Monate, ein Quartal, an. Grundsätzlich sind auch andere Zeiträume möglich – auch ein Einzeldurchlauf ist durchführbar. Es ist jedoch zu beachten, dass im Unternehmen eine zeitliche und inhaltliche Synchronisation der Zyklen sinnvoll sein kann, vor allem, wenn die Zielwelt ebenfalls koordiniert ist. (Breyter, 2022)

Jeder Zyklus startet mit dem Planning. Anschließend werden die Weeklys durchgeführt. Den Abschluss bildet dann ein Review/Retro. (Wozny, 2021)

6.3.5. Prozesselement *Planning*

Beim Planning werden die Parameter für den beginnenden Zyklus festgelegt. In Form eines Workshops arbeiten die Teammitglieder des jeweiligen Teams oder der Organisationseinheit unter der Moderation der Teamleitung zunächst an den Objectives. Hierbei sind ggf. die Moals und die Vorgaben der Hierarchie (über die Hierarchiestufen bis in die Teams kommuniziert) bzw. der Teamleitung zu berücksichtigen. Im Ergebnis stehen Objectives für das Team bereit, auf die die einzelnen Mitglieder mit Hilfe ihrer individuellen Key Results hinwirken. Die Formulierung der Key Results bildet das Ende des Plannings, so dass im Ergebnis für den Zyklus die Objectives und Key Results feststehen. (Wozny, 2021)

6.3.6. Prozesselement *Weekly*

Die Weeklys finden in der Regel wöchentlich zu einem einheitlichen Termin und für einen kurzen Zeitraum, beispielsweise eine halbe Stunde, statt. (Wozny, 2021) Ein anderer Rhythmus kann sinnvoll sein – auch 14-tägige Weeklys sind möglich. Letztlich wird der Rhythmus durch die Aufgabenstellung determiniert. Im Rahmen des Weeklys gibt jedes Teammitglied den aktuellen Stand seiner Zielerreichung und den Zielerreichungsgrad kund. Hierzu werden die Key Results der einzelnen Teammitglieder, beispielsweise mit einer Meta-Planwand, oder elektronisch mit einer Tabelle, visualisiert und mit dem Zielerreichungsgrad versehen, um Transparenz und einen Dialog zu ermöglichen. Auch notwendige Anpassungen in der Zielformulierung finden hier statt. Zusätzlich kann ein Austausch über Unterstützungsbedarf oder Probleme bei der Zielerreichung stattfinden. (Qadria, 2023)

6.3.7. Prozesselement *Review/Retro*

Im Review /Retro wird im Rahmen eines Workshops im Team auf den abgelaufenen Zyklus geblickt. Hier findet der jeweilige Zyklus auch sein Ende. Diese Rückschau findet auf zwei Ebenen statt. (Qadria, 2023)

Das Review befasst sich mit den inhaltlichen Themen des vergangenen Zyklus. Fragen können sein:

- Wie hoch war der Zielerrichtungsgrad?
- Was hat bei der Zielerreichung geholfen?
- Was hat die Zielerreichung gehemmt? (Weber, 2020)

Die Rückschau sollte strukturiert erfolgen. Hierzu gibt es in der Literatur zahlreiche Methoden, die helfen, einen geeigneten Rahmen zu schaffen, die notwendigen Informationen zu sammeln, Einsichten zu gewinnen, mögliche Maßnahmen festzulegen und den Workshop abzuschließen. Als Beispiele sind die Starfish-Methode und die 4-L-Retrospektive genannt. (Heidemeyer, 2023)

Im Retro hingegen wird auf die organisatorischen Inhalte des letzten Zyklus zurückgeschaut, um auch hier für die folgenden Zyklen Verbesserungen vornehmen zu können. Hier werden Fragen gestellt wie:

- War der Zyklus gut organisiert?
- Was kann im Zyklus besser organisiert werden? (Weber, 2020)

Auch das Retro kann strukturiert erfolgen.

Ziel ist es, aus dem vergangenen Zyklus inhaltlich und prozessual für die nächsten Durchläufe zu lernen. (Wozny, 2021)

Abbildung 6.3: Zyklus-Darstellung als agiler Prozess für Teams
Quelle: eigene Darstellung

6.3.8. Prozesselement *Team*

Auch wenn in der klassischen Form OKR der Zielsteuerung für das Gesamtunternehmen und auf unterer Ebene für Organisationseinheiten dient, so kann die Methode auch für jede andere Form von Teams genutzt werden. Beispielsweise für Leitungsteams, Projekt- und Arbeitsgruppen oder für Organisationsübergreifende einmalige Aktivitäten. Allerdings sollte die Struktur die Elemente der OKR-Methode berücksichtigen, etwa die moderative und orientierende Rolle der Teamleitung. (Lammert, 2022)

Ob die OKR-Methode geeignet ist, hängt letztlich von der Aufgabenstellung ab. Die OKR-Methode ist eher für kreative Aufgaben oder Umsetzungsaufgaben, also Aufgaben, die eine intensive Zusammenarbeit und einen intensiven Austausch erfolgen, geeignet. In der Literatur finden sich daher auch andere, alternative Methoden zur Zielsteuerung.

6.4. Alternative Methoden zur Zielsteuerung

Einen groben Überblick über Alternativen liefert die folgende Darstellung:

Tabelle 6.1: Zielsteuerungssysteme

	MBO	Teilen	OKR
Ziele	Ziele werden vereinbart Mitarbeiter muss dann Ziele erreichen, Leistungsziele	Ziele in Zielkarte festgehalten, eigenverantwortliche Weiterentwicklung und Zielerreichung, Operationalisierung der Unternehmensziele aus der Planung, vorwiegend Leistungsziele	Fokus auf Zielen, eigenverantwortliche Weiterentwicklung und Zielerreichung, mögliche Zielhierarchie zur Orientierung (Moals, Os) Leistung und/oder Entwicklungsziele
Zeitrahmen	Fester Zeitrahmen	Fester Zeitraum	Fester Zeitraum
Zieler-reichung	Zielerreichung 100 %	Zielerreichung 90 % – 100 %	Zielerreichung 60 – 70 %
Leistungs-bewertung	Leistungsbeurteilung anhand der Zielerreichung	Leistungsbeurteilung ohne Ziele	Leistungsbeurteilung ohne Ziele
Wirkungs-richtung	Top down	Teamvorgaben aus Planung, Verteilung Bottom-up mit Coaching	60 % Top down, 40 % Bottom-up
Anker-punkt	Ziele der Führungskraft	Zielkarte	Moals, Os
Fokus	Run	Run	Change

Quelle: eigene Darstellung

Eine gemeinsame Eigenschaft der gezeigten Zielsteuerungssysteme ist eine Wirkung für einen festgelegten Zeitpunkt. Ferner werden in allen Systemen Ziele zur Leistungssteuerung genutzt.

Die Unterschiede in den meisten Abgrenzungspunkten finden sich vorwiegend im Grad der Gestaltungsmöglichkeiten.

Management by Objectives (MBO), auf Deutsch „Führung durch Zielvereinbarung", stimmt die vereinbarten Ziele der einzelnen Mitarbeiter auf die Unternehmensziele ab, so dass sich die Teammitglieder bei der Arbeit motiviert und eingebunden fühlen. Das Management-by-Objectives-Modell wurde erstmals von Peter Drucker in seinem 1954 erschienenen Buch „Die Praxis des Managements" vorgestellt. Peter F. Drucker konzentriert sich auch auf die Überwachung der Leistung von Teammitgliedern mithilfe von Tools zur Berichterstattung und Leistungsbeurteilungen (Asana, 2022).

„Teilen" hingegen ist keine wissenschaftliche Managementmethode. Diese Vorgehensweise entspringt der verbreiteten Handhabung der Zielsteuerung in Vertriebseinheiten von Banken. Für diesen Artikel wurde die Beschreibung der Methode von RMW (Unternehmensberatung aus Zürich) genutzt, die in der Untersuchungssparkasse in den Vertriebseinheiten eingesetzt wird. Teilen verbindet Elemente von MBO und OKR und dient der eigenverantwortlichen Verteilung der Teamziele auf die einzelnen Teammitglieder. (Weber, 2019)

OKR weist den größten Gestaltungsspielraum für die Teammitglieder auf und eröffnet eine Erweiterung des Steuerungsgedankens in den Bereichen Change und Entwicklung. (Lammert, 2022)

6.5. Anwendung in einer Sparkasse

Zunächst stellt sich die Frage, wieso sich die Untersuchungssparkasse überhaupt mit dem Thema Zielsysteme auseinandergesetzt und was eine Veränderung bzw. Modernisierung des alten Zielsystems notwendig gemacht hat.

Das bislang genutzte Zielsystem war in der inhaltlichen Ausgestaltung verhältnismäßig frei und konnte je nach Aufgabenstellung der Teams variiert werden. Außerdem war die Zielerreichung mit der (Leistungs-) Bewertung der Mitarbeiter verbunden und wurde in (Halb-) Jahresgesprächen zwischen Mitarbeiter und Führungskraft besprochen.

Im Rahmen einer Führungskräfte-Tagung wurde unter anderem das Zielsystem hinterfragt. Dieses System wurde als veraltet und in Teilen auch als unfair empfunden, denn

- die Verbindung von Zielsystem und Bewertung verhinderte ambitionierte Zielsetzungen, da der Schwerpunkt die Zielerreichung war,
- die geringe Frequenz der Gespräche (zweimal pro Jahr) ließen Energie und Fokus und damit die Wirkung ambitionierter Ziele nicht entstehen und
- die starre, für ein Jahr festgelegte, Zielvereinbarung war nicht flexibel, da eine reaktive, zeitnahe Anpassung nicht möglich bzw. vorgesehen war.

Aufgrund der Ergebnisse der Führungskräftetagung ließen die Verantwortlichen der Sparkasse mit Hilfe einer Unternehmensberatung neue Wege der Zielsteuerung suchen.

Um nun die Besonderheiten in der Untersuchungssparkasse zu berücksichtigen, musste auf die Unterschiedlichkeit der Aufgabenstellungen in den Organisationseinheiten und Teams in einer Sparkasse eingegangen werden. „In immer mehr Unternehmen häufen sich parallele Modi der Arbeitsteilung. Exemplarisch dafür sind die Begriffe aus dem Finanzsektor, in dem die Manager zwischen ‚Run the Bank' und ‚Change the Bank' unterscheiden. Im Modus ‚Run the Bank' werden das Tagesgeschäft erledigt und die Kernprozesse verbessert. Dagegen zielt der Modus ‚Change the Bank' darauf ab, die Grundlogik zu verändern. Damit ist das Geschäftsmodell gemeint, also die Art und Weise, wie für Kunden Wertschöpfung erbracht wird." (Cachelin, 2015)

Auch die Aufgabenart der jeweiligen Organisationeinheiten in der untersuchten Sparkasse unterscheidet sich in dem jeweiligen Anteil von Aufgaben zwischen Alltagsgeschäft und strategischen oder prozessualen Aufgaben. Während die Vertriebseinheiten vorwiegend Aufgaben aus dem Tagesgeschäft wahrnehmen, nimmt der Anteil der strategischen Aufgaben in den Stabseinheiten zu. Die Ziele der Zielsteuerung in den jeweiligen Organisationseinheiten sind folglich ebenfalls von der Aufgabenstellung abhängig.

Wenn nun der Aspekt hinzugenommen wird, dass die Zielsteuerung auch Ziele beinhalten kann und soll, die die Mitarbeiterentwicklung betreffen, dann ist die Zielsteuerung auch ein Führungsinstrument – so, wie es in der Führungskräftetagung vermisst wurde.

Es musste eine neue Idee zur Zielsteuerung gefunden werden, die geeignet war, Fokus und Energie strukturiert auf ein Ziel zu steuern und gleichzeitig motivierend zu wirken.

Als Lösung wurde OKR durch die begleitende Unternehmensberatung (RMW, Zürich) vorgestellt und getestet. Zunächst wurde in zwei Stabsabteilungen OKR als Pilot und in zwei Filialen eine von der Unternehmensberatung angepasste OKR-Variante, genannt „Teilen", testweise eingeführt. Nach ersten positiven Erfahrungen wurde OKR auf das Gesamthaus ausgerollt.

Die Erfahrungen aus den Reviews und Retros nach einem Jahr und drei Zyklen machten eine erneute Auseinandersetzung mit OKR notwendig. Die Rückmeldungen aus den Reviews und Retros zeigen die Erfahrungen der jeweiligen Teams. Die Erhebung erfolgte in den Reviews und Retros mit Hilfe der folgenden Fragestellungen im Rahmen eines Workshops:

- Wovon brauchen wir mehr?
- Wovon brauchen wir weniger?
- Was können wir weglassen?
- Was sollen wir genauso weitermachen?
- Was können wir neu machen?

Die Review-Ergebnisse wurden vom Autor zusammen mit einem Bereichsleiter der Untersuchungssparkasse gesichtet und strukturiert. Im Folgenden werden die wesentlichen Aussagen, zunächst übergreifend und allgemein und hiernach getrennt nach Review (inhaltlich) und Retro (prozessual) sowie jeweils nach positiven und negativen Äußerungen, zusammengefasst.

6.5.1. Allgemeine Einschätzung

Die erste Euphorie, mit der OKR begonnen wurde, ist abgeebbt. Die Attraktivität der Methode war in den Teams nicht immer hoch, da sie oft als „on top“ empfunden wurde, vor allem, wenn der Eindruck entstand, dass durch OKR das Alltagsgeschäft vernachlässigt wurde. Zudem war der Nutzen von OKR nicht hinreichend klar. Es zeigt sich ein gemischtes Bild, das insbesondere durch die unterschiedliche Aufgabenstellung der Teams in den jeweiligen Organisationseinheiten geprägt war. Während die Vertriebseinheiten auch vorwiegend Vertriebsschwerpunkte in ihren Zielen abbildeten, wurden in den Stabseinheiten eher Entwicklungsschwerpunkte gesetzt. Positiv wurden die Erweiterung des eigenen Handlungsspielraums und die Möglichkeit gesehen, in den Weeklys voneinander zu lernen.

Die allgemeine Einschätzung wurde für die gesamte Sparkasse wie folgt zusammengefasst:

Abbildung 6.4: Gesamtfazit des ersten Gesamtzyklus

Wie bewerten Sie die Lust und Energie, mit der Sie das Ziel erreichen wollten? 😐😐😐	Wie bewerten Sie Ihren Fokus auf das Ziel? 😐😬😬	Wie bewerten Sie Ihre Beharrlichkeit, am Ziel zu arbeiten? 😒😬😬

Quelle: Ergebnis-Präsentation (Untersuchungssparkasse)

6.5.2. Inhaltliche Rückschau – Review

In der inhaltlichen Rückschau wurden positive Einschätzungen zur Zielsteuerung, zu den Ergebnissen und zur Wirkung von OKR zusammengetragen.

Der Weg von Moals über Objectives zu Key Results war aus Sicht der Teilnehmer hilfreich, da mit ihm eine Orientierung zur Formulierung von Key Results vorhanden war und der Zielfokus auf die Gesamthausziele gerichtet war. Positiv bewertet wurde zudem, dass sich die Zielerreichung zwischen 80 % und 90 % für die meisten Mitarbeitenden, die jeweiligen Teams und das Gesamthaus bewegte. Die Ziele (Key Results) haben die Mitarbeitenden motiviert und das hohe Ambitionsniveau führte zu positiven Erfahrungen. Ebenso wurde die Möglichkeit einer zwischenzeitlichen Zielanpassung als nützlich und motivierend empfunden. Insgesamt wurde OKR trotz hoher externer Belastungen (beispielsweise durch Corona) gelebt. Hierbei wurde die Qualität der Key Results verbessert und die Umsetzung der Key Results als wichtiger gesehen als die Wertung durch einen Prozentsatz.

Auch die Ergebnisse führten zu Zufriedenheit. So konnten mit Key Results Grundlagen (Vorarbeiten) für künftige Aufgaben gelegt werden. Zudem konnte stringent an Themen, beispielsweise an konkreten Ertragszielen oder persönlichen Entwicklungszielen, gearbeitet werden. Dabei haben die Regelmäßigkeit und die Struktur der Weeklys geholfen.

OKR zeigte eine positive Wirkung auf die Zielerreichung im Vertriebssteuersystem (Zielkarten). Die Formulierung von gemeinsamen Key Results mehrerer Teammitglieder hat sich ebenfalls bewährt. In Stabsbereichen wurden oft Themen aus „man-müsste-mal-Listen“ aufgegriffen und umgesetzt. Auch für spezielle Themen, wie beispielsweise die Einführung eines neuen Mitarbeiters oder eine zentrale Kampagne, konnte mit Hilfe der Key Results konsequent umgesetzt werden.

Demgegenüber wurden für die Zielsteuerung (sowohl für Objectives als auch Key Results), zur Wirkung von OKR im Allgemeinen auch negative Erfahrungen zusammengetragen. So waren Objectives oftmals so offen oder allgemein formuliert, dass sich die Teammitglieder für die Formulierung von geeigneten Key Results konkretere und trennschärfere Objectives zur Orientierung gewünscht hätten. Dazu passt auch, dass die Führungskräfte bzw. das Team sich auch bei der Formulierung von geeigneten Objectives schwertaten.

Ebenso war die Erarbeitung von Key Results eine große Herausforderung, denn neue Impulse, die richtige Zielgröße und Zieltiefe war oftmals schwer zu finden und („smart“) zu formulieren.

So war es schwierig, auch die Begeisterung für OKR und die Qualität der Key Results aufrecht zu halten. Zudem bestand teilweise die Neigung, alltägliche Aufgaben als Key Results zu formulieren, anstatt Key Results als motivierende, begeisternde Ziele zu formulieren. Insgesamt haben sich die Mitarbeitenden und Führungskräfte mehr Freiheiten bei der Ausgestaltung der Objectives und Key Results gewünscht.

Auch die Wirkung von OKR wurde als abgeschwächt empfunden, da der Zyklus-Durchlauf insgesamt als „schlecht" wahrgenommen wurde. Die Zielerreichung war in einigen Bereichen nicht zufriedenstellend bzw. sehr heterogen, da es beispielsweise Teams gab, bei denen Weeklys mitunter abgesagt wurden, um das Alltagsgeschäft nicht zu hemmen.

Letztlich war der Umgang mit OKR immer noch heterogen und es wurden auch die Ziele unterschiedlich gehandhabt. Zudem stellte sich heraus, dass eine Abstimmung der eigenen Ziele (Objectives und Key Results) mit den Zielen anderer Teams und Organisationseinheiten erfolgen sollte – ebenso mit Aktionen außerhalb der OKR- und Zielsteuerungswelt, beispielsweise Vertriebskampagnen.

6.5.3. Organisatorische Rückschau – Retro

Positive Rückmeldungen ergaben sich im Retro für die Bereiche Weekly, Wirkung und allgemeine Organisation.

Der 14-tägige Rhythmus der Weeklys wurde als geeignet und, da er als fester Termin eingerichtet ist, als hilfreich eingeschätzt. In den Vertriebseinheiten wurde ein Rhythmus von vier Wochen als positiv angesehen.

Eine verbesserte Verinnerlichung des Umgangs mit OKR bei Teams und Teamleitungen sowie mehr Routine in den Weeklys werden positiv gesehen. Hierbei hat das Review bzw. Retro geholfen zu lernen. Auch wurde der letzte Zyklus als bisher bester Zyklus (organisatorisch) eingeschätzt und eine gute Wirkung durch stringentes Arbeiten z. B. an Verbundertragszielen erkannt.

Ebenso wurde die allgemeine Organisation von OKR als verbessert wahrgenommen. Dabei war zunächst ein Leitfaden sehr hilfreich, der vom Personalbereich der Sparkasse erstellt wurde und den Teamleitungen an die Hand gegeben wurde. Auch der Wechsel von vier auf drei Zyklen im Jahr wurde positiv gesehen. Eine Herausforderung bestand (bedingt durch Corona) in der Abkehr von Weeklys in Präsenzform hin zur Nutzung von Skype. Dieser Wechsel wurde positiv aufgenommen, da so eine stärkere Stringenz entstand. Auch das Abwechseln in der Moderation, bei der jedes Teammitglied als Moderator in Frage kommt, hat sich bewährt, da so die Identifikation mit OKR erhöht wurde.

Es wurde positiv bemerkt, dass das OKR-Weekly für sich alleinsteht und nicht mit anderen Themen vermischt bzw. als Teammeeting genutzt wird.

Insgesamt bestand inzwischen eine größere Sicherheit im Ablauf von OKR. Und es wurde vorgeschlagen, OKR auch zu nutzen, um OE-/teamübergreifende Ziele zu steuern und um ganz allgemein Veränderungen zu bewirken.

Negative Rückmeldungen wurden zu den Themenbereichen allgemeine Organisation, Ziele, Weeklys, Zusammenarbeit zwischen Teams und OKR in der Hierarchie geliefert.

Die allgemeine, übergreifende Organisation von OKR könnte verbessert werden. So waren die Zyklenwechsel, also der Übergang von Review/Retro in das nächste Planning nicht gut terminiert und unklar und wurden daher als holprig empfunden. Es wurde außerdem vorgeschlagen, die Weeklys wieder in Präsenzform durchzuführen, um die Dynamik zu erhöhen. Gleichzeitig wurde der entgegengesetzte Vorschlag gemacht, also die Durchführung per Skype beizubehalten.

Zur Zielsteuerung wurde vorgeschlagen, die Objectives und Key Results unter den verschiedenen Teams auszutauschen bzw. transparent zu machen, um die Zusammenarbeit zu verbessern. Auch wurde die Idee formuliert, Team-Key Results zu bilden, also ein Key Result für mehrere Teammitglieder.

Für die Weeklys wurde angemerkt, dass oft die Zeit für die Durchführung gefehlt habe. Daher bestand die Forderung, sie einzuhalten und eben nicht ausfallen zu lassen. Auch wurde gefordert, Weeklys monatlich stattfinden zu lassen. Ein Vorschlag war, eine teamübergreifende Gast-Teilnahme an Weeklys zu ermöglichen.

Die Zusammenarbeit zwischen den Teams könnte durch teamübergreifende Unterstützung bei der Bearbeitung von Key Results vertieft werden. Auch teamübergreifende Objectives wurden zur Verbesserung der Aufgabenerfüllung und Zusammenarbeit vorgeschlagen.

Zur Frage, wie OKR in der Hierarchie ausgestaltet sein sollte und ob und wie Objectives kaskadiert (also entlang der Hierarchieebenen ausgestaltet) werden sollen, bestand Unsicherheit. Denn Fragen wie beispielsweise „Gibt es entlang der organisatorischen Hierarchie auch eine „O-Hierarchie"? oder „Zu welchen Objectives bilden Führungskräfte ihre Key Results?" waren nicht beantwortet.

Insgesamt waren die Ergebnisse aus den Reviews und Retros sehr heterogen. Während einzelne Themen durch Regelung festgelegt werden konnten, beispielsweise die Zyklus-Dauer, konnten andere Themen wie die Zielfokussierung (Vertriebsziel oder Entwicklungsziel) schwieriger begriffen werden. Es wurde deutlich, dass es noch Unklarheiten über die Ausgestaltung von OKR, aber auch konzeptionelle Defizite bei der Versuchssparkasse gab. Eine Anpassung von OKR sowohl konzeptionell als auch in der Handhabung erschien notwendig.

6.6. Weiterentwicklung von OKR und Erstellung eines Konzepts für die Sparkasse

Ein Zweierteam aus der zweiten Führungsebene der Untersuchungssparkasse, bestehend aus dem Autor und einem weiteren Bereichsleiter, hat sich mit OKR auseinandergesetzt. Hierbei wurde OKR generell und in seinen Elementen noch einmal in Frage gestellt und mit anderen Zielsteuerungssystemen aus der Literatur im Rahmen eines Workshops mit Hilfe einer Gegenüberstellung verglichen. Zunächst wurden die Gestaltungsräume zu OKR beleuchtet, um danach ein Konzept zu erstellen, das die Anwendung von OKR speziell für die Untersuchungssparkasse zum Ergebnis hat. Sodann schloss sich eine Würdigung an, um den Erfolg der Anpassungen messen zu können. Diese Arbeiten wurden in drei Schritten durchgeführt:

- Erste Arbeitssitzung
  - Festlegung der Vorgehensweise
  - Sichtung aller Unterlagen
  - Formulierung von Arbeitsaufträgen
- Abarbeitung der Arbeitsaufträge
  - jeder einzeln
- Zweite Arbeitssitzungen
  - Zusammenstellung der Ergebnisse
  - Dokumentation der Ergebnisse im Konzeptpapier (Präsentation)

6.6.1. Gestaltungsräume

Zunächst konnte festgestellt werden, dass bereits die Gestaltung der Moals sehr variabel sein kann. Moals werden auf Basis des normativen Rahmens des Unternehmens formuliert und berücksichtigen dabei die Strategie, die Planung, den Kultur- und Werterahmen, die Vision, die Mission, die Zielbilder sowie externe Anforderungen. Diese Basis lässt eine große Breite für die Formulierung von Moals zu, was es nicht leicht macht, geeignete Moals zu finden. Die Formulierung kann dann in Form von moderierten Workshops oder (mit Hilfe eines Leitfadens), beispielsweise durch die Geschäftsleitung, erfolgen. Die so gefundenen Moals stellen dann die Grundlage für die Erarbeitung von Objectives dar. Da – je nach Aufgabenstellung der Teams – Objectives auch ohne Moals formuliert werden können (beispielsweise bei speziellen

Aufgaben, wie Kampagnen), können Moals entbehrlich sein. Wenn auch ohne die Orientierung an Moals geeignete Objectives gefunden werden können, beispielsweise durch andere Orientierungsmöglichkeiten (wie bei der Orientierung an der Teamleitung), ist die Erarbeitung von Moals obsolet.

Da OKR für die Zielsteuerung der Aufgaben sowohl für formelle als auch für informelle Teams und Arbeitsgruppen geeignet ist, können Objectives auch für beide Teamarten formuliert werden. Die Gestaltung der Objectives unterscheidet sich dann in ihrem Freiheitsgrad, denn die formellen Arbeitsgruppen (beispielweise Organisationseinheiten oder Projektgruppen) sind mit ihren Aufgaben in die bestehenden Prozesse des Unternehmens eingebunden. Daher erfolgt die Formulierung in Anlehnung an die (wenn vorhanden) Moals. Demgegenüber helfen informelle Gruppen, beispielsweise Arbeitsgruppen oder informelle Teams mit einer Sonderaufgabe, aufgrund ihrer Aufgabe bei möglichen Moals nicht.

Neben der Orientierungsmöglichkeit durch Moals kann mittels Eingreifens oder Beteiligung der Teamleitung Einfluss auf die Gestaltung von Objectives genommen werden. Auch der Einflussgrad kann variiert werden. Die Bandbreite erstreckt sich dabei von der Vorgabe von Objectives bis hin zur freien Formulierung durch die Teammitglieder. Die Wertung der Geeignetheit der Objectives obliegt weiterhin der Teamleitung.

Die Formulierung von Objectives ist also in Abhängigkeit der Aufgabenstellung des Teams in ihrem Freiheitsgrad hinsichtlich der Richtung als auch hinsichtlich des Konkretisierungsgrads variabel gestaltbar.

Die Beiträge der einzelnen Teammitglieder, die Key Results, werden durch die Teammitglieder eigenständig formuliert und wirken auf die Objectives. Obschon die Key Results konkret („smart") formuliert werden sollten, ergeben sich auch hier in der Ausgestaltung Freiräume. So kann beispielsweise ein Key Results ein Aufgabenziel oder aber ein Entwicklungsziel sein. Ein Teammitglied kann sich ein oder mehrere Key Results vornehmen und bearbeiten. Auch ist es möglich, dass zwei oder mehr Mitglieder ein gemeinsames Key Result formulieren.

Die Gestaltung der Weeklys kann ebenfalls variiert werden. Zunächst ist der Rhythmus des Treffens variabel. Ein wöchentliches Treffen hat sich bei Projekt-Gruppen ebenso bewährt wie bei Teams mit Sonderaufgaben. Andererseits kann für Teams mit einem hohen Anteil an operativen Aufgaben auch ein 4-wöchiger Rhythmus geeignet sein. Ein 14-tägiger Rhythmus kam bei der Untersuchungssparkasse am häufigsten vor.

Ferner kann das Weekly hinsichtlich der Dauer und der Inhalte variiert werden. Wenn im Rahmen des Weeklys alleine die aktuellen Umsetzungsstände der

Key Results besprochen werden, ist die Dauer kürzer, als wenn ausführlich über die aktuellen Stände der Key Results mit etwaigen Hemmnissen gesprochen wird. Je nach Aufgabenstellung des Teams sollte die Dauer des Weeklys variiert werden.

Eine Integration des Weeklys in ein Teammeeting, beispielweise als separater Tagesordnungspunkt, ist ebenfalls möglich.

Der letzte untersuchte Gestaltungsraum beschäftigt sich mit der Art des Teams beziehungsweise der Aufgabengruppe. Die Elemente von OKR lassen sich auf jede Art von Gruppe in der Untersuchungssparkasse übertragen. Nicht nur für Organisationseinheiten, die sich aus der Aufbauorganisation ergeben, sondern für jedes Team, das durch gemeinsame Aufgaben entsteht – sei es als formelle oder informelle Gruppe – sollte die OKR-Methode für die Zielsteuerung geeignet sein. Selbst wenn zwei Mitarbeitende eine gemeinsame, vielleicht auch befristete, Aufgabe haben, könnten sie OKR als Aufgaben- und Zielsteuerungsmethode nutzen.

Insgesamt kann je nach Aufgabengestaltung und Teamgestaltung OKR für die Steuerung der Ziele und teilweise auch für die Steuerung der Aufgaben genutzt werden und geeignet sein. Die Variationsmöglichkeiten, die möglich sind, können dann im Rahmen der Gestaltungsräume aufgebaut werden. Für die Untersuchungssparkasse sollte hierzu ein Konzept dienen.

Es wurde deutlich, dass innerhalb der Untersuchungssparkasse OKR nicht als isoliertes Instrument gesehen werden kann, sondern in die bestehenden Instrumente zur Führung und Zielsteuerung implementiert werden muss. Zunächst ist OKR auch ein Führungsinstrument. Daher muss für das Konzept der Sparkasse auch eine Einordnung in die Führungsinstrumente der Sparkasse erfolgen. Zudem ist zur Orientierung eine Abgrenzung von OKR zu anderen Aufgabenarten hilfreich, damit die Ausrichtung von OKR als Instrument der Ziel- und Aufgabensteuerung deutlich wird. Hiernach können die konzeptionellen Elemente für die Untersuchungssparkasse festgelegt werden.

In der untersuchten Sparkasse steht OKR nicht als einziges Führungsinstrument zur Verfügung. Die Führungsphilosophie der Sparkasse verbindet im Wesentlichen vier Führungsinstrumente, um einerseits in der Beziehung Führungskraft – einzelner Mitarbeitender (Impulsgespräche und Bewertungsgespräche) und andererseits in der Beziehung Führungskraft – Team (Erfolge feiern und OKR) wirksam zu werden. Es wird deutlich, dass die Performance als Teamleistung bei der Leistungserbringung im Vordergrund steht, was durch die OKR-Methode Unterstützung findet.

Abbildung 6.5: Führungsinstrumente der Untersuchungssparkasse
Quelle: eigene Darstellung

Die Einbettung in die Aufgabenarten der Sparkasse macht deutlich, dass auch hier die OKR-Methode nicht die einzige Art von Aufgabenbearbeitung zur Zielerreichung ist.

Den größten Anteil der Aufgabenbearbeitung nimmt naturgemäß die alltägliche Arbeit, eingebettet in die hierarchische Struktur der Sparkasse, ein. Hierbei liegt die Art der Arbeit zwischen den Gegenpolen operativer Arbeit und strategischer Arbeit. Während bei Vertriebs- und Produktionseinheiten meist die operativen Aufgaben überwiegen, ist bei Stabseinheiten der Anteil strategischer Aufgaben höher.

Im Gegensatz zu hierarchisch eingebetteten Aufgaben liegt die Teamzusammenstellung bei Projektgruppen (oder anderen Arbeitsgruppen) außerhalb der Aufbauorganisation des Unternehmens.

OKR kann nunmehr als drittes Element angesehen werden, da diese Methode eine Aufgabenbearbeitung in jeder Teamzusammenstellung ermöglicht, sowohl innerhalb oder außerhalb der Aufbauorganisation als auch in einer Mischform. Zudem kann OKR nicht nur als eigenständiges Aufgaben-Steuerungsinstrument genutzt werden, sondern auch mit seinen Gestaltungselementen als Zielsteuerungssystem für die anderen Arbeitsformen dienen.

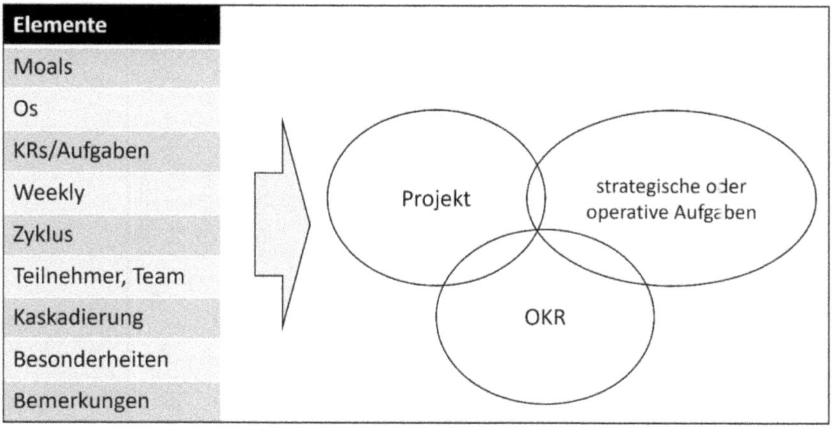

Abbildung 6.6: Aufgabenarten
Quelle: eigene Darstellung

Das Konzept für die konkrete Anwendung in der Versuchssparkasse muss nun die Elemente der OKR-Methode für die unterschiedlichen Team-Zusammenstellungen und Aufgabenstellungen ausgestalten und damit anwendbar machen. Hierbei sind für alle Teams, die Teamleitungen und alle Führungskräfte die konzeptionellen Ideen zur Anwendung in der Sparkasse handhabbar zu machen. Hierzu sollen neben dem eigentlichen Konzept zwei Hilfsmittel dienen, eine Anwendungsmatrix und ein Reglersystem.

Mit Hilfe der Anwendungsmatrix werden für die Elemente der OKR-Methode eine Ausgestaltung für mögliche Team- und Aufgabenzusammenstellungen aufgezeigt und die Gestaltungsvarianten dargestellt. Es handelt sich dabei nicht um eine feste Regel, sondern um eine Orientierungshilfe.

Im Original weist die Matrix zur Orientierung zwei zusätzliche Spalten auf, in denen für zwei bekannte „Musterunternehmen" ebenfalls die Ausgestaltungen der OKR-Elemente abgebildet sind.

Es zeigt sich, dass vor allem Unterschiede im Fokus der Aufgaben- und Zielerreichung festgehalten sind, aber auch, dass für Arbeitsgruppen und Projekte die Nutzung von OKR geeignet erscheint. Zudem wird deutlich, dass die einzelnen Gestaltungsräume immer noch variabel bleiben.

Daher ist ein Hilfsmittel, welches die Gestaltungsräume handhabbar macht, nützlich. Ein Reglersystem, das den Gestaltungsraum zwischen (teilweise

Tabelle 6.2: Anwendungsmatrix der Untersuchungssparkasse

Elemente	Team Vertrieb	Team Stab	Arbeitsgruppe, OE-übergreifend	Projekt
Moals	geben Orientierung	geben Orientierung	bedingt relevant	nicht relevant
Os	als „Teilen" ersetzt durch Zielkarte; Os bleiben möglich und wirken auf die Zielkarte	Formulierung von Leitung und Team (Orientierung: 60 zu 40 %)	O oder Aufgabe (Was) wird gemeinsam formuliert, Hutträger moderiert	Projektziele, Meilensteine (Was)
KRs/Aufgaben	KR zu Team-Os -> in der Kette wirksam auf die Zielkarte	KR zu Team-Os	KRs/Aufgaben (Wie) der Einzelnen werden formuliert	Aufgabenplanung (Was)
Weekly	regelmäßige Treffen (gerne wöchentlich)	regelmäßige Treffen	regelmäßige Treffen, z. B. wöchentlich	regelmäßige Projekttreffen
Zyklus	4 Monate	4 Monate	Dauer der O-Aufgabe	Dauer des Projekts
Teilnehmer, Team	OE in Markt, Vertrieb	OE in der Marktfolge, im Stab	Umsetzungsteam aus mehreren OEs; Freiwillige	Projektteam, Projektmitglieder
Kaskadierung	nein, Vertriebsschwerpunkte möglich	nein	nein	nein
Besonderheiten	relevant für die Zielkarte, abgeleitet aus der Planung	relevant ist der Effekt	Einzelprozess	Einzelprozess; bei agilen Projekten besonders organisiert
Bemerkungen	Fokus: run, Vertriebserfolg, Entwicklung	Fokus: Change, Entwicklung	Fokus: Umsetzung	Fokus: Change, Umsetzung

Quelle: Konzept der Untersuchungssparkasse

ambivalenten) Gegenpolen aufzeigt, wurde daher dem Konzept als Bestandteil hinzugefügt.

Zunächst sind allgemeine Regler zu nennen, die die Organisation von OKR im Unternehmen betreffen und entsprechende Orientierung geben sollen:

dienstlich	–	privat
Kreislauf	–	Prozess
Entwicklung	–	Leistung
Flexibilität	–	Sicherheit

Dann sind Regler zur Gestaltung der Objectives und Key Results hilfreich, um treffende und geeignete Ziele formulieren zu können:

run	–	build	(the bank)
run	–	build	(my competence)
normale Arbeit	–	add on	
Zielkarte	–	andere Ziele	(Zusammenspiel)
KRs/Os alleine	–	gemeinsam	(zusammen, helfen)
Os nur für den Zyklus	–	Zwischen-Os	
von oben	–	von unten	(Objectives)
Kaskaden	–	einzeln	
Ziele „vereinbaren“	–	sich Ziele vornehmen	

Die Aufzählungen sind nicht abschließend und können ergänzt werden. Dennoch geben sie hinreichend Hilfestellung und Orientierung.

Um die Umsetzung der OKR-Methode in der Untersuchungssparkasse beurteilen zu können, musste zunächst ein geeigneter Maßstab gefunden werden. Hierzu wurden als Maßstab die Wirksamkeit und der Nutzen für das Unternehmen als qualitative Merkmale genutzt.

Die Wirksamkeit wurde für die Wirkung auf die Gesamtsparkasse, aber auch für die Zielbereiche Objectives und Key Results betrachtet. Darüber hinaus wurden Fragen gestellt, die die Wirksamkeit der Beiträge im Rahmen der Reviews/ Retros erhoben:

- Wo konnte ich am meisten erreichen?
- Welchen Effekt konnte ich erzielen?

- Wurde jeder einzelne Beitrag als wichtig erkannt?
- Wurde in den Reviews und Retros eher nach „richtig, falsch“, oder nach „anders, hilft“ gefragt?

Darüber hinaus wurde ein Controlling zu den OKR-Prozessen und zur Wirksamkeit zu festgelegt, welches die jeweiligen Teamleitungen für die Durchführung der OKR-Methode verantwortlich macht und für die Gesamtsparkasse eine zentrale Stelle als „Hüter des Systems“, nämlich den Personalbereich, benennt, um die Nutzung der OKR-Methode als Führungsinstrument zu begleiten.

6.7. Schlussfolgerungen und Empfehlungen

In der Untersuchungssparkasse wird als Führungsinstrument (neben anderen Instrumenten, wie beispielsweise Impulsgespräche und Bewertungsgespräche) auch OKR zur Zielsteuerung und zur Mitarbeiterentwicklung genutzt. Zudem wird auch bewusst eine Trennung von Zielerreichung und Bewertung herbeigeführt. OKR als Führungsinstrument in der Untersuchungssparkasse erzeugt Fokus, Beharrlichkeit und Energie bei den Teammitgliedern, um Leistung und Entwicklung zu steigern und zu steuern.

Die OKR-Methode ist für die Zielsteuerung und als Führungsinstrument in einer Sparkasse geeignet (Forschungsfrage 1). Der Nutzen von OKR für die Untersuchungssparkasse erstreckt sich dabei vom einzelnen Mitarbeitenden bis hin zum Gesamtunternehmen. So hilft die Methode jedem einzelnen, seinen Betrag einzubringen und seinen Fokus auf bestimmte Aufgaben zu richten. Für die einzelnen Teams werden Themen (sowohl Alltagasthemen als auch Sonderthemen) greifbar und eine strukturierte Aufgabenumsetzung wird möglich. Die Unternehmensleitung kann mit Hilfe von Moals oder vorgegebenen Objectives den Fokus für das Gesamtunternehmen steuern und Wirkung erzielen. Für die Sparkasse als Ganzes ist die OKR-Methode eine Umsetzungshilfe, ein Zielsteuerungsinstrument und ein Führungsinstrument, mit dem Effekte erzielt werden können.

Die OKR-Methode ist mehr als ein System zur Zielsteuerung und kann auf nahezu jedes Unternehmen und jede Aufgabenstellung angepasst und dort genutzt werden (Forschungsfrage 2). OKR kann durch seine agilen Bestandteile zur Zielsteuerung und für die Aufgabenbearbeitung genutzt werden und ist dabei nicht nur auf die Strukturen des jeweiligen Unternehmens beschränkt, sondern ist für jede Art von formeller und informeller (Arbeits-) Gruppe geeignet. In modifizierter Form kann die OKR-Methode auf andere Sparkassen,

Banken und Unternehmen und Aufgabenstellungen, beispielsweise auf Projekte, übertragen werden. Möglich wird dies durch eine individuelle Ausgestaltung der Prozesselemente zu OKR. Diese können auf die jeweilige Aufgabenstellung und auf das jeweilige Zielsystem modelliert werden.

Als Hilfsmittel können auch hier jeweils eine individuell zu erstellende Anwendungsmatrix und ein eigenes Reglersystem (nach dem Beispiel der Untersuchungssparkasse) genutzt werden:

Elemente	AUSPRÄGUNGEN (Beispiele, erweiterbar)	Team A	Team B	Arbeitsgruppe	Projekt
Moals	• keine • zur Orientierung • als Vorgabe				
Os	• Vorgabe durch Teamleitung • gemeinsame Formulierung durch Team • gemischte Form z.B. (60/40) • Projektziele				
KRs/Aufgaben	• jedes Teammitglied für sich • gemeinsame KRs				
Weekly	• regelmäßig, wöchentlich • anderer Rhythmus • bei Bedarf				
Zyklus	• regelmäßig alle drei Monate oder andere Dauer • Einzeldurchlauf (z.B. bei einem Projekt)				
Teilnehmer, Team	• formelle Gruppe • informelle Gruppe • Projektgruppe				
Einbindung in Hierarchie	• Einbindung • keine Einbindung				
...					
Besonderheiten	• Einbindung in agile Projektorganisation • O = Ziele aus Zielkarten				
Bemerkungen	• Fokus, besondere Vorgaben				

Die Zuordnung wird individuell festgelegt

Abbildung 6.7: Muster für die Erstellung einer Anwendungsmatrix
Quelle: eigene Darstellung

Im Rahmen künftiger Forschungen könnte untersucht werden, inwieweit die Methode des Morphologischen Kastens bei der Erstellung der Anwendungsmatrix genutzt werden kann.

Für die Erstellung eines Reglersystems könnten ebenfalls Techniken der Ideenfindung, beispielsweise Mindmaps oder die 6-3-5 Methode, genutzt werden. Das Reglersystem ist frei gestaltbar und gibt Orientierung.

Regler für die Organisation von OKR im Unternehmen:

Zyklen	-	Einzelprozess
Entwicklung	-	Leistung
Flexibilität	-	Sicherheit
Geschwindigkeit	-	Genauigkeit
Zielsteuerung nur im Team		Zielsteuerung unternehmensweit
…	-	…

Regler zur Gestaltung der Zielelemente:

Moals		keine Moals
run	-	build (company)
run		build (competence)
normale Arbeit	-	add on
Zielkarte		andere Ziele
KRs/Os alleine	-	gemeinsam
von oben	-	von unten (Os)
Kaskaden	-	einzeln in Teams
Ziele „vereinbaren“		sich Ziele vornehmen
…	-	…

Abbildung 6.8: Muster für die Erstellung eines Reglersystems

Quelle: eigene Darstellung

Literatur

Asana. (2022, 23. Juni). *Management by Objectives: Erklärung, Vorteile und Nachteile!* https://asana.com/de/resources/management-by-objectives

Becker, W., Feichtinger, C. & Betz, L. (2020). Agiles Management in der Unternehmensführung – eine empirische Untersuchung. *Der Betriebswirt,* 61(2), S. 103–117. https://doi.org/10.3790/dbw.61.2.103

Breyter, M. (2022). *Agile Product and Project Management: A Step-by-Step Guide to Building the Right Products Right.* Apress.

Cachelin, J. L. (2015, 12. November). Change oder Run the Bank? Neue Rollen sind gefragt. *blog.hrtoday.ch.* https://blog.hrtoday.ch/change-oder-run-the-bank-neue-rollen-sind-gefragt/

Changement (2022). OKR: Strategiearbeit in Zeiten der digitalen Transformation. *Changement!,* 9/2022, S. 66 (GBI-Genios Deutsche Wirtschaftsdatenbank GmbH).

Die.agilen (2022). *Referenzen – unsere zufriedenen Kunden, die.agilen GmbH.* https://www.die-agilen.de/okr-referenzen

Doerr, J. (2018). *OKR – Objectives & Key Results: Wie Sie Ziele, auf die es wirklich ankommt, entwickeln, messen und umsetzen.* Vahlen.

Heidemeyer, C. (2023, 2. Februar). *54 spaßige Retrospektive Methoden für agile Teams in 2023.* Echometer. https://echometerapp.com/de/retrospektive-methoden

Klein, N. (2022). *OKR in der Sparkasse Neuss, Konzept für die Untersuchungssparkasse.* Nicht öffentliche Unterlage.

Kudernatsch, D. (2019). OKR – eine neue Management-Wuderwaffe. Controller Magazin, November/Dezember 2019.

Lammert, S. (2022). OKR – „Zeit schaffen" als Schlüssel zum Erfolg – Objektives & Key Results: Start with Time. *projektmagazin,* 20/2022.

Niven, P. R. & Lamorte, B. (2016). *Objectives and Key Results: Driving Focus, Alignment, and Engagement with OKRs.* Wiley.

Praz (2022). Einrichten von OKRs. In *Verknüpfen Sie Technologie mit Ihren langfristigen Geschäftszielen.* Berkeley, Kalifornien: Apress https://doi.org/10.1007/978-1-4842-8208-3_9

Qadria, M. F., Raudaschl, W. & Wanjek, L. (2023). *So geht agile Führung mit 'Objectives and Key Results' (OKR). Wie eine Unternehmensvision erfolgreich auf Team- und Mitarbeiterebene synchronisiert wird.* Deloitte GmbH Wirtsc haftsprüfungsgesellschaft. https://www2.deloitte.com/de/de/pages/financial-services/articles/okr-framework.html

Weber, R. M. (2019). *Planungsworkshop Objektive.* RMW Consulting. Präsentationsunterlage – nicht öffentlich.

Weber, R. M. (2020). *Planungsworkshop Review/Retro.* RMW Consulting. Präsentationsunterlage – nicht öffentlich.

Wozny, S. (2021, 3. September). *OKR – Objectives and Key Results.* RUHR PM. http://www.ruhrpm.de/agilitaet/okr-objective-key-results

Innovatives Wissensmanagement
Innovative Knowledge Management

Herausgegeben von Prof. Dr. Dr. Dr. habil. Bernhard F. Seyr

Band	1	Bernhard F. Seyr (Hrsg.): Innovations- und Wissensmanagement in der Praxis: Konzepte, Forschungsergebnisse und Fallstudien. Innovation and Knowledge Management in Practice: Concepts, Research and Case Studies. 2020
Band	2	Bernhard F. Seyr (Hrsg.): Multidisziplinäre Perspektiven im Innovations- und Wissensmanagement. Multidisciplinary Perspectives in Innovation and Knowledge Management. 2021
Band	3	Bernhard F. Seyr (ed.): Applied Innovation and Knowledge Management in Organizations. Angewandtes Innovations- und Wissensmanagement in Organisationen. 2022.
Band	4	Daniela Hofmann: Personalmanagement in Non-Profit-Organisationen unter besonderer Berücksichtigung der Motive und Haftungsrisiken Ehrenamtlicher. Eine empirische Untersuchung in den Ländern Deutschland und Österreich. 2023.
Band	5	Bernhard F. Seyr (ed.): Systemic Knowledge Management and Social Challenges. Systemisches Wissensmanagement und soziale Herausforderungen. 2023.

www.peterlang.com

www.ingramcontent.com/pod-product-compliance
Ingram Content Group UK Ltd.
Pitfield, Milton Keynes, MK11 3LW, UK
UKHW021833100926
8556IPUK00004B/311